Health and Illness

European Monographs in Social Psychology

Series Editor HENRI TAJFEL

E. A. CARSWELL and R. ROMMETVEIT
Social Contexts of Messages, 1971

J. ISRAEL and H. TAJFEL
The Context of Social Psychology: A Critical Assessment, 1972

J. R. EISER and W. STROEBE
Categorization and Social Judgement, 1972

M. VON CRANACH and I. VINE
Social Communication and Movement, 1973

in preparation

H. GILES and P. F. POWESLAND
Social Evaluation through Speech Characteristics

J. INNES
Bias in Psychological Research

J. K. CHADWICK-JONES
Social Exchange Theory

SERGE MOSCOVICI
Social Influence

EUROPEAN MONOGRAPHS IN SOCIAL PSYCHOLOGY 5
Series Editor HENRI TAJFEL

Health and Illness
A Social Psychological Analysis

CLAUDINE HERZLICH
École Pratique des Hautes Études,
Paris, France

Translated by
DOUGLAS GRAHAM
University of Durham, England

1973

Published in cooperation with the
EUROPEAN ASSOCIATION OF EXPERIMENTAL
SOCIAL PSYCHOLOGY
by
ACADEMIC PRESS *London and New York*

ACADEMIC PRESS INC. (LONDON) LTD.
24–28 Oval Road
London NW1

US editions published by
ACADEMIC PRESS INC.
111 Fifth Avenue
New York, New York 10003

Library of Congress Catalog Card Number: 73–9463
ISBN: 0–12–344150–1

PRINTED IN GREAT BRITAIN BY
WILLMER BROTHERS LIMITED,
BIRKENHEAD

Preface*

This book is based on a study conducted in France in the 'sixties. The intention now is not to "adapt" it or to "refashion" it in any way. The study has a specific historical and cultural context: we use in it extensively the concept of "social representation" deriving from Durkheim's work which is perhaps less familiar to the English than to the French. There have been, since this book was written, some important new developments in the social analysis of medicine and of illness. For these reasons, it seems useful to precede the text with a brief discussion of three problems.

The first concerns the relationship between these new developments and our approach to the problem of the lay conception of health and illness. Would this be different today from what it was when the study was conducted? It seems important to note, in this context, the increasing tendency of the new research to focus on the role of medical knowledge and practice in *creating* definitions of illness and even the reality of illness. But as these medical definitions increase in importance, mainly because they contribute so much to the structuring of laymen's ideas about illness, they tend to lose their unquestioned acceptance as sources of incontrovertible evidence. They no longer appear to us as a reflection or the deciphering of "natural" reality; instead, they tend to be interpreted as arising themselves from complex processes in which a number of factors interact, at least some of which are amenable to analysis by the social scientist.

It is becoming increasingly clear that lay conceptions and "biases" are amongst the factor which to some extent influence medical thought and practice. Or at least that they function as a "filter" helping to select the "objective reality" of the pathology presented to the physician. Therefore, it is probable that recent research developments have tended to accentuate even further the importance, stressed in this book, of studying the popular conceptions of illness and health, not only in their

*Translated by Henri Tajfel.

relation to medicine, or their discrepancies from it, but also for their own sake.

The second point has to do with our use of the concept of social representation. Even today, most of the relevant research takes the form of an analysis of variables, such as membership of a social class or of an ethnic group, which are associated with the perception of types of symptoms or with attitudes towards specific illnesses. This enables us to draw conclusions about the social or cultural variability of the notions of health and illness: it does not, however, tell us very much about how these notions are constructed and elaborated. Similarly, although there is general recognition today of the importance of the socially shared value connotations of illness, very little is known about social communication concerning illness which serves as a meeting point between individual experience and social values. It would seem that this is where the concept of social representation becomes a factor in our understanding of the processes of the social construction of reality.

The development of an analysis of illness in terms of its social definition as a form of deviance is relevant, at a different level, to the same point. The notion of illness considered as a "label" attributed to certain states is closely linked to the functioning of social representations. But these are not the limits of this functioning. Illness may appear not only as a form of deviance but also as having a symbolic function, as bearing witness to the threats from the aggressive outside world of which the sick person is then seen as a victim.

These *post hoc* justifications of our approach are not intended as an attempt to conceal its defects and shortcomings. To begin with, it has been difficult to provide a precise definition of the links between what we call "social representations" and the *individual* behaviour of people who are ill or healthy. Are the modes of social communication which enable us to grasp these representations a form of construction of reality which, in some way, determines behaviour? Or are they no more than self-contained verbal attempts to rationalize behaviour?

The study examined here concerns these questions. They are not easy to answer. But the recent development in the United States, and later in other western countries, of ecological movements and pressures of public opinion is obviously relevant; these new preoccupations reflect a close correspondence between, on the one hand, some of the major themes of social representation—such as those of an individual constrained or attacked by a noxious society, of the confrontation between healthy and unhealthy, between "natural" and "artificial"— and, on the other hand, collective behaviour in the form of a social and political movement.

It is this correspondence between representations and social behaviour which, it seems to us, gives the present study a significance which goes beyond its specific socio-cultural context. There has been an historical continuity since the times of Rousseau and of the early reformers during the industrial revolution who were preoccupied with conditions of life in the new factories and in the growing cities. This has been a continuity of a certain kind of social representation. When an individual talks about health and illness, he also talks about something else: the nature of his links with his environment, physical and social, as well as aspects of social organization. Thus, although we would not wish to claim that a study of representations provides us with the means of understanding the rise of a social movement, it provides us at least with its correlates and reflections which are profoundly rooted in collective conscience.

Paris, 1973

CLAUDINE HERZLICH

Foreword

The practice of interrogating the public on a wide range of topics has become common during the past decade. The publication in the press of the results of opinion surveys is an indication of the large number of investigations carried out for private or public bodies. These surveys or inquiries constitute items of information and tools of influence when they present what is claimed to be the attitude of the majority; they also form the basis for decisions or for the postponement of decisions. No study ever provides clear-cut conclusions and one can always find support either for an immediate decision or for waiting for more detailed investigations. Generally it is not difficult to work out replies to questions in terms of percentages. It is more difficult to fathom what these percentages represent. What conclusions can be drawn when 60 per cent of businessmen say there is going to be a recovery in the market? Does it mean they intend to invest? Does it reflect a tendency which they have themselves observed? Or are they drawing conclusions on the basis of an analysis of the market, founded on their experience and their business foresight? In other words, are the responses in such an inquiry models of behaviour, reflections of reality or examples of a particular kind of cognitive system? Some years ago I chose the third alternative, and showed that these responses reflect an autonomous process of psychological organization, and express a social representation. In taking up this neglected concept of Durkheim's, my intention was to counteract the disadvantages of an excessively static and fragmentary view of the universe of social discourse and to emphasize the possibility of a scientific analysis of what is commonly called common sense. Since then, there has been an increasing amount of research on ideas and representations concerning adolescents, urban life and economic behaviour. These studies, however, do not seem to represent any conceptual or methodological turning point. They give the impression of a different nomenclature superimposed upon a fundamental similarity of meaning between terms like opinion or attitude, and image or social representation. It is important to note the differences, since they concern both the phenomena observed and their theoretical implications. Opinion, or attitude, represents both a socially approved pronouncement which a subject accepts, and a position on some controversial social problem. We asked a group of subjects: "Can psychoanalysis have a beneficial effect in relation to criminal behaviour?" Sixty-nine per cent replied "Yes", 23 per cent "No" and 8 per cent were not sure. At first sight this would appear to indicate what the people concerned thought on the issue at the time of the inquiry. However, the context, the criteria of judgement and the categories of thinking which underly these criteria have not been taken into account. Most texts have described opinion as being relatively unstable, concerned with circumscribed specific items; in short, opinion is admitted to be a stage in the formation of attitudes and stereo-types. Its fragmentary nature is generally accepted. To put it more generally, the notion of opinion implies: (1) reaction on the part of individuals to some object presented from outside, complete in itself, independent of the actor, his intentions or his predispositions; (2) a direct connection with behaviour, in so far as judgement is concerned with a social stimulus and constitutes a kind of anticipation or internalized picture of future action.

In this sense, an opinion, like an attitude, is regarded entirely from the point of view of response, as a "preparation for action", or verbal representation of known behaviour; and hence, opinion is accorded predictive value, since we deduce what a person is going to do from what he says.

The notion of "image" does not differ much from that of opinion, at least in respect of its basic presuppositions and its usage. It would appear to be used to indicate a more complex or more coherent organization of judgements or values. In a persuasive little book, Boulding[1] proposes the establishment of a science of eiconics devoted to the study of images. This suggestion indicates an obvious gap in social psychology, which should include the study of these social images. It also indicates a renewal of interest in cognitive phenomena and a dissatisfaction with current notions in this field. Anyone who pursues this suggestion, however, will find that it involves a return to very old ideas. As in the case of any psychological mechanism, it is emphasized that an image has intellectual, affective and behavioural components.

[1] Boulding, K. (1956). "The Image". University of Michigan Press, Ann Arbor.

[1] Moreover, it is presented as an internal reflection of an external reality, a mental reproduction of that which exists outside the mind. "An individual normally carries in his memory a collection of images of the world in its various aspects. These images are combinatorial constructs analogous to visual experiences. They are interdependent to varying degrees, both in the sense that the structure of some images can be inferred or predicted from the structure of others, and in the sense that changes in some images produce imbalance tending towards change in others."[2] We may regard these images as "mental sensations" or impressions which objects and people leave in our brain. Like sensations or perceptions, these "cognitive atoms" or copies of external stimulation combine to produce different perceptions or images. Thus their function is purely selective. "Images serve as screens for the selective reception of new messages, and they often control the perception and anticipation of those messages that are not completely ignored, rejected or repressed."[3] Here, they do not appear to be in any way different from opinions or attitudes, as these are envisaged in classical psychological theories.

When we speak of social representations, we generally start from a different viewpoint. First of all, there is no implication of any clear-cut division between the outside world and the inner world of the individual (or group); subject and object are not regarded as functionally separate. An object is located in a context of activity, since it is what it is because it is in part regarded by the person or the group as an extension of their behaviour. For example, any judgement of a political party depends upon the experience of the person who makes the judgement, and his definition of the party and of the political set-up. Not to recognize the power of our capacity for representation to create objects and events is like believing that there is no connection between our "reservoir" of images and our capacity for imagination. Sociologists and psychologists who see in this reservoir only faithful copies of external reality appear to deny this obvious capacity of the human species. In associating the existence of an object with opinion concerning it, we have adopted

[1] Scott, W. A. (1965). Psychological and social correlates of international images, in "International Behaviour (Ed. H. Kelman), pp. 71–103. Holt, Rinehart and Winston, New York.
[2] Deutsch, K. W. and Merrit, R. L. (1965). Effects of events on national and international images, in "International Behaviour" (Ed. H. Kelman), p. 132. Holt, Rinehart and Winston, New York.
[3] Deutsch, K. W. and Merrit, R. L. (1965). Effects of events on national and international images, in "International Behaviour" (Ed. H. Kelman), p. 134. Holt, Rinehart and Winston, New York.

the view that to form a representation of something is to apprehend stimulus and response at one and the same time. The response is not a reaction to the stimulus, but, up to a point, constitutes the origin of the stimulus. What does this really mean? Normally, if a person pronounces a negative judgement on Marxism, we conclude that he takes a position with respect to a body of knowledge and a movement, clearly defined in the eyes of all. But if we look closer, we can see that Marxism is apprehended as an ideology in such a way as to permit this negative judgement. As a result of the operation by which the object is constituted, a judgement of value may appear as a judgement of fact. If a social representation is a "preparation for action", it is so because of this process of reconstruction and reconstitution of the elements in the environment. Its outstanding function is to make behaviour meaningful and to integrate separate behaviours into a whole. The points of view of individuals and groups are then seen as much from the point of view of communication as from that of expression. In general, images and opinions are indexed, studied and considered exclusively as indications of the position or scale of values of an individual or a community. In reality, an individual or a community *communicate* their ways of seeing things to their interrogator and prepare themselves intellectually for this purpose. A subject who answers a question in the course of an inquiry is not simply selecting a response category, he is giving us a message. He is aware that faced with another investigator, or in different circumstances, the message would be coded differently. Such variation does not imply that the response is less genuine, nor that there is any kind of Machiavellian attempt to hide a "true" opinion. It is simply a matter of the interaction situation which emphasizes this or that aspect of the problem and requires the use of a language adapted to the transitory but symbolic relationship associated with this particular occasion. We may note here that, according to Heider, representation involves an expectation or interchange in terms of customary relations between social groups or individuals. "The problem of consciousness, of openness to the world, or, if you will, of representations, gains a special significance if we consider the relations and interactions between people."[1] The concepts of image, opinion and attitude do not include the associations and anticipations to which they give rise. Individuals or groups are envisaged in a static way, as they make use of the information circulating in society, and not as they create such information. Because they determine both the object and the related judgement, and because they interact with one another, social representations are cognitive systems with a logic and language of their own and a pattern of implication, relevant to both values and concepts, and with a characteristic kind of discourse. They do not represent simply "opinions about", "images of" or "attitudes towards", but "theories" or "branches of knowledge" in their own right, for the discovery and organization of reality. They continually go beyond what is immediately given in the form of existing organization or ready-made classifications of facts or events. The classification of facts and events which they involve is influenced by, for example, legal, scientific or medical classifications, but is nevertheless different and original. This divergence is justified; for a representation is a representation held by someone as well as a representation of something. The relations which form or find expression here are also reflected in the representation. Thus town dwellers or country dwellers take apart and recombine biological and medical statements in accordance with the positions they hold with regard to society as a whole, the medical profession, etc. The map of social interaction can be read from images, knowledge and symbols. To form a representation is not to select and complete an entity objectively given by reference to its subjective aspects. It is to go beyond this, to construct a theory to facilitate the task of identifying, programming or anticipating acts or sets of events.[2] Rather than a kind of shadow cast upon society by a particular kind of experience or knowledge, a social representation is a system of values, ideas and practices with a twofold function; first, to establish an order which will enable individuals to orientate themselves in their material and social world and to master it; and secondly to enable communication to take place among the members of a community by providing them with a code for social exchange and a code for naming and classifying unambiguously the various aspects of their world and their individual and group history. In this, social representations differ from the notions we have already considered and from the phenomena corresponding to them.

These preliminary notes have been too long, but their justification is that they supply a background to the significant and original work of Mme Herzlich. Readers will find no questionnaires, scales or statistical

[1] Heider, F. (1958). Consciousness, the perceptual world and communication with others, *in* "Person Perception and Interpersonal Behaviour" (Eds R. Tagiuri and L. Petrullo), p. 27. Stanford University Press, Stanford, California.
[2] Jaspers, K. (1954). "Psychologie der Weltanschauungen". Springer, Berlin.

tests. Mme Herzlich explains why this is so and defends herself against the charge of not having used such techniques. But one may well wonder whether, in view of the current state of knowledge, she could have been justified in doing so. Her aim, in which she has succeeded admirably, was to reveal in detail the notions, the categories and the kind of language in terms of which, in our society, health and illness are distinguished. By a series of associations and interpretations, Mme Herzlich has reconstructed their context and the series of meanings which enable us to see what people are really talking about when they talk of healthy or sick people; they are concerned with the relations between the individual and society, and between society and nature. Health behaviour and the classification of pathological or pathognomic indices acquire their unique significance in the light of these relations. What we read in the present work on fatigue and on eating habits indicates that this is so. Mme Herzlich does not treat health or illness as entities which can be recognized and defined in unambiguous terms, and does not attempt to assess people's reactions to them, nor the effects which they produce in people's minds, but rather re-creates them as results of social processes, of cognitive elaboration and of the continual verbal interaction within our community. Thus, we can observe and understand the processes involved in the development of a social representation and the function of the social representation itself in the constitution of reality, so that it represents valid knowledge because of the agreement among those who accept it. The present research has pursued its aim clearly and with sound results. It constitutes a serious contribution of lasting value to the psychosociology of our culture, i.e. the aspect of our culture which is least studied. In my view, the contribution of the present study is much greater than that of many other studies which, although they use more sophisticated methods and may be in a technical sense more professionally "respectable", have been less well adapted to the object of their inquiry and therefore make a less genuine contribution to the progress of science.

1968   SERGE MOSCOVICI

Laboratory of Social Psychology, École Pratique des Hautes Études, Paris.

Contents

Foreword   v

Introduction   1
  The psychosocial view of illness. Anthropology and sociology
    of medicine   1
  The social representation of health and illness. Problem and
    methodological orientation   10
  The study   13

PART 1

**Chapter 1   The individual, the way of life and
the genesis of illness**   19
  'Way of life'   20
  Individual factors   23

Chapter 2   Nature, constraint and society   28
  Way of life and its meanings   28
  Health and nature – the artificial and the unhealthy   31
  A world without illness, or, health as a constraint   38

Chapter 3   Mechanisms and usage   41
  A mechanism: toxicity   41
  Perception and anticipation   44
  Some reflections on the genesis of health and illness   47

PART 2

Chapter 4   Health and illnesses   53
  Health and its forms   55

Chapter 5   Illnesses – dimensions and limits   65
  Illnesses and their classifications   65
  Illness in health: the intermediate state of fatigue   69

CONTENTS

Chapter 6   The sick and the healthy   74
  Death   75
  Physical realities and behavioural aspects   76
  The sick and the healthy   85

PART 3

**Chapter 7   The social representation of health and
            illness**   91
  Genesis, conditions and conduct   91
  Hygiene   95

**Chapter 8   Conceptions of illness and illness
            behaviour**   104
  Illness as destructive   105
  Illness as a liberator   114
  Illness as an occupation   119

Chapter 9   The invalid and his identity   126
  Conclusion   133

Appendix 1   141

Appendix 2   142

  Destructive illness   142
  Illness as a liberator   142
  Illness as an occupation   148

Bibliography   151
Author Index   155
Subject Index   157

Introduction

The psychosocial view of illness. Anthropology and sociology of medicine

What do health and illness mean for us and what is their significance for the members of our society? Their meanings emerge partly through individual experience and partly from the views current in society which reflect its values. To be ill or well would appear at first sight to be essentially an individual rather than a shared experience. And yet this kind of incommunicability involves some relation to others; a person is ill or well not only in himself, but also for society and as a function of society.

Thus illness, initially a matter of direct experience, becomes something which is learned. A child seems not to grasp what illness is nor to understand its future significance in his life; he has to learn to locate his experience in a framework of social explanations and rules. The "doctor–patient game" in particular would appear to fulfil this function. The adult learns from society to be ill. This learning process starts with the name which the doctor gives the illness. Then come prescriptions, which are rules of action, and the encounter with institutions— the hospital and Social Security. For both doctor and patient, and for the recipient of assistance from Social Security in his dealings with the administration, roles are differentiated and norms of conduct emerge. From the point of view of society, the patient is different from the healthy citizen.

If we wish to investigate the social definition of health and illness, we must examine the way the individuals in our society view and experience this pattern of values, social norms and cultural models, and the way in which the notion of social entities called "health" and "illness" develops and crystallizes, both logically and psychologically. By this means we can approach the conception which each individual has of reality, its organization and its meaning. But, since this conception itself plays a part in shaping behaviour and is a source of behaviour, in investigating it we are also studying one of the sources of reality.

An approach of this kind must inevitably be conditioned by the view current in our culture by which health and illness are regarded as psychosocial as well as organic entities. The recent tendency to include in the category of illness forms of personal and social maladjustment, hitherto regarded as material for which only a social or legal approach was appropriate, would seem to provide a further indication that illness has ceased to be exclusively something physical to be studied only in physical terms. This psychosocial point of view is accepted by a number of doctors and finds expression, in various forms, both in medical textbooks and in the daily press. It is beginning to find its way into institutions through, for instance, the reform of the medical curriculum and the training of hospital personnel. And finally it underlies various kinds of approach to the phenomenon of illness.

Such a point of view is not as new as it may appear. At the very least we can say that, in its most general sense, it runs through the whole history of medical thinking. We can distinguish between theories based on the objective examination of physical signs of disease and theories which view health and illness as modes of relationship—equilibrium and disequilibrium—between man and his environment, involving human factors, ecological aspects and social structure. From one point of view, the development of scientific medicine would appear to represent the triumph of the physically centred approach; many medical historians regard Hippocrates as the founder of medicine because he invented the clinical method, the observation of the patient, his symptoms and his body. But we should remember that Hippocrates also took note of the effect of climate, air, water and earth on the prevalence of certain diseases.

In the course of the centuries, the "body orientation" came to predominate and we have the development, from the 16th century, first of anatomy and then of physiology. Later came the use of notions from physics and chemistry. There was, however, also another line of development revealed, for example, in an interest in strange diseases such as that shown by Paracelsus, and reinforced, according to Sigerist (1955), by the discovery of "new lands in which colonists encountered diseases previously unknown". (See, for example, the analysis by Valabrega,

1962, chapters 6 and 7.) Later, in the 18th and 19th centuries, there was an upsurge of a veritable medical geography: the authors, for example, August Hirsch (quoted by Sigerist, 1955), drew maps of the distribution of diseases in space and time. During this period, philosophers and doctors also devoted their attention to the connection between disease and social conditions. Campaigns for better hygiene and improved living conditions were frequent (see Dubos, 1961, chapter 4). One fact in particular shows that these approaches to illness were closely associated with a particular view of the nature of pathology. During the 19th century, with the triumph of Pasteur's theories, medical geographies were abandoned as the view of the nature of pathology changed. Although the existence of geographical factors could not be denied—there really is a geography of disease—they appeared unimportant and research became almost wholly concerned with the study of the microbic agent itself. Similarly, theories of hygiene changed their orientation as Pasteur's germ theory became more popular, emphasis no longer being placed on the intrinsic importance of living conditions.

Recently there has been a reaction against the exclusively organic and "ontological" view of illness which has taken the form of a systematic study of the psychosocial factors which are involved in illness and medical practice. Three aspects of this reaction may be distinguished.

1. Because of its interest in the nature of the phenomena and its preventive and therapeutic aims, it falls within the sphere of medicine. Psychosomatic medicine, however ambiguously it may sometimes be defined, is concerned with the psychological as well as the organic causes of illness; social medicine and social psychiatry are aimed at prevention and cure.

2. A second aspect is the interest in the cultural relativity of conceptions and forms of behaviour in the field of health and disease. In particular, anthropology has shown us, in studies of more primitive societies than our own, the cultural variations in medical myths, beliefs and practices, and the ways in which these are related to the overall pattern of values in each culture.

3. The third aspect concentrates on illness in our own society, studying it as a form of social reality and a kind of social behaviour. This is the starting point of the sociology of medicine.

The present study falls somewhere on the borderline between the second and third aspect, being partly anthropological and partly psychosociological in its approach.

ANTHROPOLOGY

There are many well-established studies of primitive medicine which have been carried out for a variety of reasons (see, for example, Rivers, 1924). It has often been thought that these have provided a suitable approach to the study of these societies, and to primitive thought itself. The aim was sometimes a practical one—to gain the acceptance of western medicine and hygiene by peoples who knew little or nothing about them. Sigerist (1955) indicates other approaches, for example, historical interest, contending that medicine as practised in existing primitive societies might cast some light upon the origins of modern medical thinking and practice. Here, a parallel is assumed between contemporary primitive societies and societies of former times. Interest has also been shown in comparing primitive medical beliefs and practice with western popular medicine and superstitions, implying that the same mental mechanisms are involved. In all these cases, the authors have, as an essential part of their task, grappled with the problem of how illness is defined in the societies concerned.

If the sociology of medicine is characterized, as we shall later show, by fractionation into sub-problems and therefore by a series of limited though genuine contributions, anthropological studies are, on the other hand, characterized by their *holistic* nature. In dealing with the cultures they are observing, the authors do not separate medical practices from the representations which contribute to their orientation. Moreover, they relate these representations to other, more general, notions and values—ideas about the universe, the gods, human relations, and good and evil.

The subject matter of these studies is crucially influenced by two basic notions. First, the representations of illness, the behaviour of the sick and their associates, and medical practice vary from culture to culture. But these variations can be systematized in certain crucial ways. Thus, we have the classic distinction between the conceptions of disease as endogenous, and as exogenous. In exogenous conceptions—also called centripetal and additive (Valabrega, 1962)—illness is caused by the real or symbolic intrusion of some object into the patient's body. In endogenous conceptions (centrifugal or subtractive), illness is caused by the magical theft of the individual's soul. Exogenous theories would seem to be used more to explain painful diseases, and endogenous theories for disorders accompanied by loss of consciousness. Exogenous theories are found particularly in America, Australia and South East Asia. Endogenous theories come from Siberia. It has also been suggested that the two conceptions may have originated in the paleolithic and neolithic eras respectively (Clements, 1932).

The second basic notion is that the representations and practices in any society are associated with the global value system of that society. Illness may be, as has been said, of magical origin, caused by the action of another man or a sorcerer. Or it may be of religious origin, produced by a god or a spirit. The essential point here is the absence of any clearly defined differences between medicine, magic and religion. The practices associated with all three of these are interlinked, just as systems of values and representations are interlinked. Illness, in the last resort, results from an offence against the gods, the dead or society, from the infringement of a taboo or a failure to observe the values of the group. And for the patient himself illness is a sanction. Moreover, the sick person, even if he is rejected, often has a sacred quality; and in many societies, the medicine man or shaman also plays the part of priest or sorcerer.

More recently, some rather different studies have appeared, concerned with problems of acculturation and resistance to change arising from the introduction of western hygiene and medicine into different cultures. Some authors (see, for example, Mead, 1954; Saunders, 1959; Carstairs, 1955; Gould, 1957) of such studies show that it is often impossible to obtain acceptance of any technique which goes against a firmly established notion in a society; others show how, in a given population, medical ideas and practices inherited with the culture intermingle with those of modern scientific medicine rather than disappearing. The problem of the relationship between representation and conduct is involved in all these cases.

It has been emphasized that some anthropological analyses might profitably be applied to our own society. Stoetzel (1960) observes that we can classify historically the main western medical theories in terms of endogenous or exogenous conceptions of disease. Exogenous conceptions predominate in certain early theories; for instance, in the Hippocratic explanation of epilepsy in which the external phenomenon of the winds is held to be the cause, in the theories concerning epidemics and contagion which emerged during the Middle Ages and the 16th century, and finally, and most notably, in the work of Pasteur. Endogenous conceptions are centred upon ideas of the resistance of the body to disease, predisposition and heredity. According to this kind of view, illness comes from man himself. Canguilhem (1943) refers to Greek medicine, for example, as dynamic and holistic. "The disease is not in some part of man, it is in the whole man and it is entirely within the man."

There are also important studies of the development of medical ideas, theories and practice in more modern times. The best of the numerous histories of medicine—for example, those of Sigerist (1943, 1955) and of Shyrock (1947)—do not separate the development of medical science from the social conditions from which it emerged, nor from its practical consequences for society. But the outstanding instances here are the definitive volumes by Canguilhem (1950) and Foucault (1961, 1963).

On the other hand, the idea suggested by Valabrega (1962) of a "modern anthropology of the facts of health and illness" has received little acceptance. But we should note the symbolic importance of these facts. This importance is attested by the volume of popular literature, the number of films and the existence of a whole folklore surrounding these themes. The fact that little progress has been made in the direction suggested by Valabrega serves to show the difficulties confronting an anthropological study of our own society.

THE SOCIOLOGY OF MEDICINE

The first publications in the sociology of medicine appeared in the United States during the 1940's, but there has been a considerable development in this field since then. An investigation by Strauss in 1957 included references to the work of 110 investigators in the field. These early publications seem most frequently to have had pragmatic aims: to contribute to the humanization of medicine, for example by making it necessary for hospital staff to acquire the rudiments of a training in the human sciences. Thus some of this work is of a very general or even question-begging nature. Although authors soon widened their perspectives, the double orientation, towards practice or towards research, still exists, as is to be expected in such a field. This double orientation would appear to reflect the distinction made by Strauss in 1957 between sociology *of* medicine and sociology *in* medicine.

In many cases, the methods and concepts of sociology have been transferred to the study of medicine. Thus, epidemiological research has been concerned with establishing relationships between health, illness, ecological conditions and social factors.[1] On the sociological side, the sociology of organizations has found the hospital a particularly suitable object for study. And finally, the study of the medical professions has appeared as a branch of the sociology of occupations. In all these cases, contributions have been substantial. Nevertheless, the limits of these studies must be recognized. For instance, epidemiological studies can establish relationships but cannot really indicate the mechanisms involved. What is needed here is an approach which will integrate social factors and psychological or psychosocial aspects. In 1953, Ruesch attempted to study not only the role played in illness by social class membership, but also the relation of illness to the social technique (dominance or submission) characteristic of the individual. The use of the concept of stress (see, for example, Hans Selye, 1956, and Mechanic's compendium, 1968, chapter 9) may also be viewed as a step in the same direction. On the other hand, studies in the medical field do not appear always to have defined a subject-matter of their own; and it has been said that the very numerous studies of the hospital have, in general, in common only the ecological framework within which they are located.

In contrast, the study of response to illness—behaviour and interpersonal relations in health and sickness—has from the start been approached with more specific perspectives. It is true that many studies of the information, attitudes or behaviour of patients, or of healthy persons towards patients and diseases, have been purely descriptive, especially studies which have attempted to establish the cultural and socioeconomic concomitants of any given knowledge, attitude or behaviour; this also applies to those which describe the various stages of illness. (Thus Lederer, 1952, describes different phases of illness—beginning, recognition, convalescence—and Balint distinguishes between the unorganized and the organized stages in illness. Barker *et al.*, 1953, uses topological concepts, while Goldstein and Dommermuth, 1961, conceive of the role of the patient in cyclical terms.) It is, however, with the idea of "illness behaviour" that the sociologist comes into his own. Illness is now defined in terms of situation and social behaviour, as well as in terms of biological reality. The notion of "illness behaviour" can be found in some psychoanalytical works. It is,

---

[1] For chronic illness, see Graham (1963) *in* "Handbook of Medical Sociology". For mental illness, there are the classic studies of Faris and Dunham (1939) and, more recently, of Hollingshead and Redlich (1958). In France, there is Bastide's (1965) synthesizing study.

however, Parsons' analysis of the roles of patient and doctor in our society which has provided the theoretical frame of reference in most of the studies (cf. Mechanic, 1960).

Psychoanalysis introduces a conception of illness and the patient centred on the notions of flight into illness and of the primary and secondary gains obtained thereby. The problems of etiology are here taken onto the individual level; to escape into illness is to escape from personal problems and social constraints. Psychoanalysis emphasizes the possible psychogenesis of disorders; the idea of illness being caused is here replaced by the idea of illness being motivated. These ideas have inspired Balint (1957) among others. Starting from the role of the person of the doctor himself and the relation with him during the process of recovery—the doctor, according to him, is the commonest form of medicine in current medical practice—he has given us a brilliant analysis of the various relational mechanisms involved in medical consultation which include the "offerings" of the patient, representing various expressions of his conflict and of his attempts to escape from it, and the "apostolic function" of the doctor who responds to them. As far as behaviour is concerned, that of the patient is dominated by introversive and regressive tendencies, of which his dependence on those around him and the exaltation of his ego are part. Some non-psychoanalytic writers (Barker *et al.*, 1953; Stoetzel, 1960) also agree with the tenor of these analyses.

Contrary to this conception, Parsons (1951, 1958) defines illness as a form of deviance which society has to control. This point of view appears to be opposed to that derived from psychoanalytical notions. The patient is distinguished not by his individual destiny, but by his position in society. Illness is viewed not from the point of view of its causation, but from the point of view of its incidence; it is no longer a result but a problem to be solved.

These two perspectives are, however, reconcilable and even complementary. It is because flight into illness is a temptation for everyone that society has to exercise control over the sick and those around them. Society therefore creates roles to be played. The doctor's role is to channel in the patient the form of deviance represented by illness. The patient's role combines regressive aspects, permitted secondary gains such as freedom from responsibility and the right to assistance, with more positive types of behaviour; for instance he has his own obligations in that he must want to get better and cooperate with the doctor in seeking a cure. For Parsons, illness is therefore not just the outcome of regressive behaviour, but is also a form of adaptive behaviour. The patient is not defined solely by reference to his deficiencies compared to the healthy man, but, like the latter, has his own social role.

It is difficult to restrict the behaviour of the patient to regressive and passive forms of behaviour without taking into consideration, as Parsons does, their positive function in a more general process of adjustment to the situation: by his clearly defined role within the society, the patient adjusts both to his illness and to the demands of society. But the limits of Parsons' analysis have also been pointed out: it is valid mainly for western societies and is limited to a certain kind and stage of illness, i.e. when there is recourse to medical care (see, for example, Freidson, 1961–1962). Valuable in that it has inspired a number of empirical studies, this analysis seems to confuse the sociological level of analysis with the level of psychological experience. Although it is very relevant for the description of quite general social expectations, it seems less adequate to deal with the actual norms and attitudes of individuals, and fails to take account of some aspects of their behaviour. Thus, the individual patient does not always accept the role which society wishes to impose upon him; he sometimes rejects it and thus becomes, as it were, deviant in his deviance. People like this are difficult patients who do not conform to the expectations of the doctor, of the patient's associates or of society.

Thus, both in Parsons' analysis and in a number of empirical studies, the actual relation of the individual to health and to illness does not appear to be clarified. In the study by Mechanic and Volkart (1961), for example, the concept of sick role does not really clarify what it is supposed to clarify. It is limited to establishing a relationship: the individual more inclined to see himself as a sick person adopts the role of patient more easily (i.e. he is more likely to consult a doctor). On the one hand, in this, as in other studies, the definition of illness behaviour in terms of recourse to medical care is perhaps too narrow. On the other hand, the study of behaviour is not clearly related to the way in which the individual sees and interprets the situation.

For Parsons, again, it is the doctor who legitimizes the illness. The role of patient thus corresponds fairly closely to medical expectation. However, the recognition of the admittedly preponderant role of the doctor and of modern medicine in the social definition of illness should not imply the almost total neglect which we find of laymen's notions (with a few exceptions, for example, Apple, 1960; Baumann, 1961). If behaviour is the result of the articulation of medical institutions and knowledge on the one hand with popular notions and attitudes on the other, the latter cannot be regarded simply as responses to a reality wholly defined from without. Attempts like that of Freidson (1961) to analyse a lay system of reference as distinct from the medical system of reference and to allow it full weight are, however, rare. But it would appear that, in addition to describing behaviour, we can advance the analysis by asking the following question: If roles become institutionalized, what conceptions of the situation of the patient in society do they correspond to for the individual?

The social representation of health and illness. Problem and methodological orientation

It is clear that in the study of the response to illness we need a psychosocial orientation centred upon the articulation of the person and the socio-cultural system. We must study, in addition to institutions and knowledge about health and illness, the attitude of the individual to these, and the meaning which they have for him. From his point of view, we shall examine the social representation of health and illness and try to understand the ideas and behaviour which they engender, and what is commonly known about them, by studying the relationship which develops between the individual, health and illness.

During the past few years, the study of social representations, for so long neglected, has been revived in France. There have been studies of the representation of a scientific theory as a means of knowing and as a basis for action (psychoanalysis) (Moscovici, 1961), of that of a social role (that of the woman) (Chombart de Lauwe et al., 1963) and of a particularly highly valued area of activity (culture) (Kaes, 1966). In each case, the study has reflected the need for a better understanding of the way in which the individual constructs social reality and orients himself towards it. Each author in fact emphasizes that the representation of a particular object forms part of the more extensive representation of the whole society. Because of this, it is always the relation of the individual to society with which we are concerned.

We must note first of all the complex nature of the psychological reality which the term "representation" indicates; the blending of concept and percept, and individual images and social norms are both involved in this mode of perceiving an object or perceiving social reality itself. In the present case, by the representation of health and illness, we mean the complex psychological elaboration by which the experience of each person and the values and information current in society are integrated into one significant image. The field is a vast one, for states of health and illness, their criteria, sick people and healthy people and their behaviour and roles, are all involved.

This image of reality can, however, be studied at two levels. It is, on the one hand, the perception and evaluation of an experience, directly influenced by the social norms, and thereby serves to influence the orientation of attitudes and behaviour. It is also the construction of an idea: the conceptualization of the experience which, reflecting the notions of health and illness, represents the cognitive counterpart of models of behaviour. Our object should be to relate these two sets of factors, the cognitive and the dynamic.

The close connection of such an image with one particular mode of social thought, science, should also be noted. The importance of medical popularization in our own society, and the eagerness of the public in this respect, are well known. Knowledge is also transmitted by other paths, one of the most important being the medical consultation. It may be wondered, then, whether the study of social representation of health and illness does not simply reduce to listing the extent of public knowledge and its sources and modes of transmission, and to evaluating their content. The problem remains, however, of trying to trace any anthropological aspects which there may be in the understanding of illness which have escaped medical knowledge. Is the representation any more than an emasculated and distorted version of the scientific models? Or can one really talk about illness without medical language? Is there a system of reference in its own right indicating the ways in which information is organized and assumes meaning for the members of a social group?

The most interesting thing about the representation in the present context, however, is its role in the construction of social reality. If individual experience acquires its meaning as a result of encounters with cultural values and models, and if it is channelled into shared conceptual categories, then here we have individual experience fusing with social reality to produce a unique entity within which communication, consensus and social norms become possible. And so we find that what we must be concerned with is the significance of health and illness for the individual in society. The social representation reflects the relation of the individual to both illness and health, as well as to society.

What we shall be concerned with is the way in which a social object takes shape for members of our society. Although we shall refer to certain social psychological processes (concerned with the genesis of behaviour towards a social object and with its cognitive organization), we shall nevertheless borrow the integrative perspective of anthropology. Similarly, although we shall start with an examination of content (that attributed to health and illness), we shall proceed to examine also the mechanisms by which the representation becomes established and its function in orienting behaviour.

Such a study must initially be tentative and exploratory, but this does not mean—at least as far as the content of the image is concerned— that we cannot have an initial framework. This framework has, in fact, been developed on the basis of an acquaintance with the psychosociological, psychoanalytic, ethnographic and historical literatures on health, illness and medicine.

Personal experience and fiction have also played their part. The main guiding principles are the following.

1. The first problems involve the criteria of the notions of health and illness and their interrelations. How are these two concepts related? Are they symmetrical? Are they mutually exclusive?

2. We shall also be concerned with ideas of the *causes* of illness and health. Are there in our society clearly definable endogenous or exogenous conceptions of illness? How are normal and pathological phenomena regarded?

3. Thirdly, there is the problem of the relation between the concepts of health and illness on the one hand, and values on the other. Is health regarded as "good"? Is illness "bad"? Is it regarded as a *fault*? Are responsibility and guilt associated with these problems in our society, and what effect does this have on the behaviour of the sick and the healthy?

4. Fourthly, how is the incidence of health and illness conceived to affect social participation? Is illness regarded as a form of *deviant behaviour*? What are the norms of behaviour for the invalid and for the healthy person?

5. Finally, what do people see as the relations between health, illness and death?

The orientation of the research led us to allow those interviewed a certain amount of freedom, since their views actually constituted the material to be observed. This meant that too closely controlled methods of observation had to be ruled out and suggested the choice of the open interview as the only technique suitable for the collection of data. The material collected is not like that in the standard type of investigation, involving the exhaustive collection of opinions or records of behaviour; nor can it take account of the deeper and more intimate aspects of experience. It does not reach the underlying unconscious reality. But it would appear to offer the individual the means of expressing in a number of ways (opinions, the information he gives, the feelings he expresses and accounts of his experience and behaviour) his image of health and illness. The interpretation of this data is aimed at integrating each of the separate items into a unified picture, as the individual himself sees it, and not in a way which would be alien to him.

The study

An extensive study of a representative sample of the French population would have been quite impracticable, and indeed was never intended. We aimed rather at an analysis of general psychological content and mechanisms than at a precise sociological description or the description of different phenomena. A further and more extensive inquiry may provide validation of the picture which we present here, and indicate the effects of relevant variables.

We interviewed 80 subjects. Half of them were professional people (all of whom had had at least some higher education); the others were middle-class, i.e. office workers, minor civil servants, craftsmen and small tradesmen, or wives of men in those occupational categories (all of whom had had primary or secondary education). Within each of these two groups, the subjects were divided more or less equally in respect of age and sex, i.e. men and women of between 25 and 40 years of age, and those over 40.

We selected these two groups—middle-class and professional people— because of the active role which it seemed reasonable to attribute to them in the genesis, transformation and renewal of ideologies in our society. The presence of a small group of people living in the country (the middle-class group includes 12 people living in a small village in Normandy) represents an admittedly very limited attempt to include a style of life variable, which may reasonably be supposed to be important in matters of health and illness.

The ill–healthy dimension was not taken into consideration, since we did not wish to define the situation of being ill or being well *a priori*. It was, however, possible to classify subjects according to the nature and degree of their experience Thus, 24 per cent of our subjects told us that they were ill at present, 13 per cent thought that they had been seriously ill, and 20 per cent had had one or more accidents.

Before the actual collection of the data, we ran a series of non-directive interviews which enabled us to select the themes which seemed relevant for the subjects of our experiment. The problem then was to translate the questions asked by the investigator into an interview guide for the actual inquiry.

This guide was developed in terms of themes to be explored rather than in terms of closely formulated questions to be asked in a particular order. The main purpose was to indicate the right procedure for each subject, and the different interview themes were not imposed on the subjects but approached differentially both in order and in formulation (see Appendix 1).

Only one standardized question was asked directly at the end of the interview.[1] "Do you think it possible that there will one day be a world wholly without illness?" This provocative question obliged each subject to take a "futuristic" attitude removed from current reality which would seem to constitute an appropriate point of view for shedding light on the problems of health and illness. There must be innumerable Utopias and scientific anticipations of the future in which health and illness play an important part. The data thus collected promised to be rewarding.

We held a second interview with 20 subjects (i.e. one quarter of those interviewed) in which we asked them to comment on a retranscription of the first interview. This was designed to minimize the element of chance in the single interview situation and to facilitate the examination of the possible effects of "maturation" of the problem in the minds of the people interviewed. This procedure was partly suggested by the observations of some subjects at the end of the interview, such as, "I think I'm going to go on thinking about these things."

[1] However, since the idea of exploring this notion only occurred to us in the course of the inquiry, the question was not put to everyone, but only to 37 subjects.

Altogether, then, our data were obtained from one hundred interviews, each lasting about one and a half or two hours. Although our study cannot be regarded as *extensive*, it would appear to have the advantage of the *intensive* nature of the data assembled.

The data gathered presented problems of analysis, partly because the material was not standardised and, consequently, heterogeneous. The latter may be accepted as inevitable during the collection of data. When it comes to analysis and interpretation, however, it must be reduced and common units of analysis found. Both the materials and the tools of analysis must be decided upon.

One basic principle is involved: the analysis of such data cannot claim to be exhaustive but must inevitably be selective. The necessary structure and order are imposed by this very fact. The selection was made on the basis of the approach adopted and of an initial clinical inspection of the data, and was aimed in three directions, defining three main content areas of analysis.

1. The themes, concepts and constructs taking account of the *genesis* of health and illness.

2. Those which take account of the *definitions*, limitations and classification of the states of health and illness.

3. Those which take account of the behaviour of the healthy and the sick, and of behaviour towards health and illness.

From this point, our problems were the classic ones of content analysis.

1. *The choice of categories of analysis and their organization* Two types of approach looked promising: (a) the analysis of the occurrence (Osgood, 1959) of certain notions or themes to enable an initial view of the data and main lines for the differentiation of content to be taken; (b) the analysis of the co-occurrence of two or more elements. In this case, what is interesting is the existence or absence of a relation between two or more elements, in addition to the nature of the elements themselves. This enables us to go beyond the simple description of content, and to approach the problem of its organization.

2. *The choice of units of analysis* The most frequently used unit of analysis was the case itself, the complete interview, especially in the analysis of the mere occurrence of simple notions or themes. But a finer unit was sometimes called for when the problem was one of understanding

the relations between two elements, and when the relative frequency of occurrence of a term, or of one notion in relation to another, or the number of references made to it seemed to indicate its importance in the social definition.

We frequently used purely qualitative analyses without numerical data. Similarly, we were sometimes concerned with the analysis of an individual case, in which clinical intuition always plays a large part. It was in the convergence of these data and these different indices that we found the possibility of their unification. Such convergence also served to indicate some degree of validity in our observations.

As a matter of fact, with social psychology at its present stage, lacking any fully rigorous and satisfactory method of observation, strict methodological unity seems neither possible nor desirable. Indeed, it is through different methods of approach that the technique of investigation may be expected to advance. Such different methods of approach have, after all, but a single end—to make us think about the social image of health and illness and try to understand it.

We have to thank Professor J. Stoetzel, who was kind enough to supervise the study. It was carried out at the social psychology laboratory at the Sorbonne, in close association with M S. Moscovici, Directeur d'Etudes at the Ecole Pratique des Hautes Etudes. Without his advice and the interest which he showed it could not have been carried through.

Our thanks are also due to Mlle M. Gluge and Mme M. Fichelet who helped in gathering the data, and to Mme Sella, who helped with the analysis. Finally, we are grateful to M Fouilhe for having obtained the financial support necessary for the study.

Part 1

1

The Individual, the Way of Life and the Genesis of Illness

Where do diseases come from? How do they originate? What is involved in illness and what is involved in health? These questions arise immediately in conversations with subjects and our first task will be to analyse the answers which they give.

Anthropologists and historians of medicine are in general agreement that causal conceptions of illness—whether popular notions or medical theories—range between two extremes. On the one hand, illness is endogenous in man, and the individual carries it in embryo; the ideas of resistance to disease, heredity and predisposition are here the key concepts. On the other hand, illness is thought of as exogenous; man is naturally healthy and illness is due to the action of an evil will, a demon or sorcerer, noxious elements, emanations from the earth or microbes, for example. Medical theories can also be classified according to their view of the relations between normal and pathological phenomena. Health and illness may be considered as radically heterogeneous, like two conflicting factors within the individual, or, on the other hand, as relatively homogeneous, like two modes of vital phenomena differing only in degree.

At various periods, in different societies and in various guises, we can see the persistence of these broad currents of thought, and often their alternation. In this respect, scientific thinking, like popular thinking, seems to consist of an infinite number of variations on the same themes.

We have also found these two themes in the thinking of the subjects we interviewed, expressed in their own words. The endogenous theme is represented by the individual and his part in the genesis of his condition. The exogenous theme is the way of life of each person.

We shall examine in turn the relations of each of these factors—the individual and his way of life—with health and illness, starting with the way of life, which would appear to play the more important part.

Actually, the picture which is obtained in this way corresponds to a kind of selective perception or schema of reality. In the complex world of health and illness, the subjects choose certain aspects at the expense of others, from among the variety of factors which they learn about by experience or from other sources. The relations among the elements chosen can then be classified under a few simple headings.

Way of life

The way of life to which such a preponderant role is assigned, it must be noted, is life in towns. In fact, it is life in Paris that its citizens without exception refer to.[1] When some of them describe life in the country, it is to contrast it with their habitual way of life; the country dwellers delineate the encroachment of urban aspects on country life. In this sense the two attitudes can be regarded as similar.

In both cases, the urban way of life is always associated with illness, and its influence always undesirable. Its effect can, however, be viewed in several ways; it varies in degree from simple "harmful effects" to "appearance of an illness". The decline in health can have various starting points. The way of life creates in the individual, or makes use of, "weak points"; its effects will be felt especially where resistance is least. "You can have a mild intestinal infection, the first signs of a stomach ulcer, slight irritation following certain food, discomfort, early symptoms resulting from a faulty way of living . . . your organism being less ready to resist, these minor signs grow into illness."

Most frequently, however, the attack is a general one. The perceptible symptoms of it are fatigue, "nerves" and premature ageing, which all indicate weakness and physical wear and tear. For the individual, they represent entry into an "intermediate state" (this notion is clarified in chapter 4) which is neither illness nor health. Subjects almost unanimously describe, often vehemently, how city life produces a world of fatigue and nervous tension. Way of life and fatigue and disturbance of nervous equilibrium are, in the last resort, synonymous for the individual. "Paris is fatigue and nervous tension, with this

[1] Of a total of 80 subjects interviewed, 68 lived in Paris and 12 in a little village in Normandy.

exhausting and rather unhealthy life." "The constant commotion isn't made to make people ordinary, they are difficult, nervous, tired; that's the truth about modern life."

The importance of notions of nervous tension and the frequent mention of feelings of anxiety indicate that the decline concerns psychic as well as organic potential, just as the intermediate state is characterized by both physical fatigue and nervousness.

Declining health and getting into the intermediate state are two aspects of a single process. They subject the individual to the same risk —they reduce his capacity for resistance and bring increased vulnerability to illness. "You could say that now, with the life we lead, certain diseases are increasing because our body no longer reacts because it no longer has enough resistance . . ." "Modern life induces a kind of fatigue which makes us ill . . . everything to do with modern work and its conditions makes us more vulnerable to most diseases."

The way of life is thus a contributory factor facilitating attack by a pathological agent. But its effect is not limited to this; the analysis provided by some, of the respective parts and the combination of different pathogenic factors in the genesis of different diseases, indicates that the way of life plays a three-fold role and is of crucial importance in various guises, not only in the development of illness, but at its very origin. Like germs, and factors other than hereditary ones, the way of life is a releaser of illness. Finally, in addition to this releasing effect, and to the facilitating effect already analysed, the way of life is related in another and more complex way to the facts of illness, i.e. it has a role which we shall call "generating". The way of life generates the pathological agents themselves. Thus, germs and the phenomena of contagion are related to the way of life. "I reckon that in life today, the possibilities of infection are too great . . . you're attacked by germs."

They are, however, sometimes thought to be less frequent or less likely to attack one in the country. "In the country, there's the air, and so the germs don't have anything like the same effect as here."

Similarly, accidents are seen as more frequent in contemporary city life. "Accidents are a disease of our modern society, car accidents and accidents at work, it's due to our mechanized life."

At a more general level, that of contemporary society, the way of life affects the form and the distribution of illness; it imposes certain particular kinds of illness, diseases of modern life, transforms diseases and creates new ones. "I have the impression that the diseases of today didn't exist in former times, just as the diseases of former times are no longer with us today. I feel we, well not we but external circumstances and social conditions, create new sources of illness which, while still being called illnesses, take more and more diverse and complicated forms."

For this subject the association between illness and way of life appears within a bigger time-cycle in which the same process proceeds indefinitely, some diseases characteristic of a way of life becoming rare while others spread. The diseases typical of modern life because more frequent than before are in particular the following.

CANCER. "Cancer I rather associate with current allergies, with very modern allergic diseases, with the physical and nervous strain we undergo in cities, and then in breathing-in the present-day atmosphere in cities."

MENTAL DISORDERS. "Mental illness, that's a disease bound up with modern life. . . . You get much more mental wear and tear; the more restless life is, the more people are mad or half mad."

The notion—if not the expression—of psychosomatic illness appears in this context; the same person in fact carries on: "I don't know whether it may not have something to do with some other diseases, diseases which might involve a psychic state; it's important in liver disease, when you are very irritated, some people when they are afraid, get jaundice. Jaundice is the beginning of liver disease."

HEART DISEASE. "Modern life brings too many worries which make people live in a certain state of anxiety, of nervous tension which can have effects on the heart and induce heart trouble."

The notion of a harmful way of life thus embraces certain particular diseases. Mental disorders, heart disease and, above all, cancer are those most frequently mentioned, but they also have a very special significance. They are, it is said, the diseases that everyone speaks of, and therefore at the heart of the process of social communication; they are the diseases which people themselves fear, and are therefore also at the heart of individual preoccupations. These two facts indicate that the diseases of modern life constitute for the members of our society the most significant picture of illness and represent illness itself for them.

The way of life may have effects in several ways. It may involve intermediate stages (deterioration of health, intermediate state, illness). These may become stabilized; people sometimes live indefinitely in the intermediate state. The logical conclusion, however, is always illness, even if this development does not actually take place. The way of life would appear to be necessarily pathogenic.

Is this strong relation entirely unidirectional? Is there no positive relation between way of life and health? An examination of themes relating to medical progress indicates that there is, and that this takes three forms: triumph over disease by cure or prevention, reduction in the infant mortality rate and increased expectation of life. Only the reduction in infant mortality is mentioned without reservations, and that is emphasized by a few people only. In the other two cases, it is as if there were a tendency to minimize the importance of medical progress which is, in some measure, dissonant with the notion of a harmful way of life. On the factual level, people declare themselves sceptical with regard to the possibilities of prevention or cure of disease. Viewed within the context of the perpetual cycle of new diseases to which we have referred, medical progress loses its absolute quality; its victory over disease is never final. Moreover, with regard to the significance attached to the phenomena concerned, the lengthening of life does not strike everybody as an indisputable gain. To prolong life is to prolong the life of aged invalids and is not, strictly speaking, a matter of bringing or improving health. "People attach too much importance to longevity . . . why live 10 years longer on drugs when you are completely worn out, when you're falling to pieces?"

On the other hand, it is often said that health is necessary to face contemporary life. It is a sort of antidote, a necessary condition for adjustment. "The rhythm of life isn't adjusted, this rhythm of life is possible for some individuals who are particularly fortunate in the matter of health . . . anyone with good health is better equipped to react to the situation, but the rest . . . they can't get away with it."

In spite of some slight contributions, the way of life does not make for health, but, on the contrary, basically works against it, while being clearly and strongly related to the incidence of illness.

Individual factors

These constitute the second group of determining factors and are of various kinds. Each of the variables used, predisposition, constitution, temperament, nature of the individual, resistance and self-defensive reaction has a specific meaning. But they are all used for the same purpose: to describe the part played by the individual himself in the genesis of his condition, whether health or illness.

A process analogous to that which we have observed in the case of the way of life is evident; individual factors are regarded in a particular light. In spite of the variety of terms used, none refers to any pathogenic action, but all rather indicate a variable capacity for resistance to disease, and therefore to the inroads of the way of life. The terms involving the idea of resistance often appear alone. They give a sort of significance to individual factors beyond any objective notion. "There is a kind of resistance in the individual, more or less strong."

Similarly, for the notions of defence and autodefence of the individual. "There are individuals who are, so to speak, defenders; there are people whose body defends itself against illness, but there are also others who do not defend themselves and are easy victims. In present-day life everything gets them down, the least thing tires them out, and it doesn't take much for people like that to fall ill."

Other terms are also used, not to describe pathogenic factors but to refer to the capacity for resistance or defence against illness. This capacity varies according to the individual, and people's constitutions range from strong to weak. "There are people who are constitutionally more or less all right but who are nevertheless much weaker than others."

Similarly with the individual's nature. "There are people who are naturally strong, they are less affected, they put up a better fight than those who are naturally nervous, less resistant."

Organism and temperament also refer to the capacity for putting up a fight. "When there is an illness, the organism must react and put up a fight." "You have temperaments which react and others which don't."

The term "temperament" is sometimes associated with the notion of a qualitative as well as a quantitative difference, i.e. with the notion of a typology. "People with a sanguine temperament are less affected than people of a nervous type; intelligent people are more affected than less intelligent people."

Finally, there may be a selective sensitivity to certain kinds of attack, points of minimum resistance. Thus we find the notion of a pre-disposition towards certain diseases. "For diseases where you have germs . . . they always say, 'There was a liability to it, the body was vulnerable to just these germs'."

But if a predisposition is sometimes necessary before an illness can develop, it is never a sufficient condition. Similarly, heredity is not always considered as a pathogenic factor (the notion of hereditary disease or disease due to hereditary factors appears only in some subjects), but as the inheritance of weak or strong points, of fragility or robustness requiring certain precautions of the individual or making certain performances possible for him. We also find references to the inheritance of temperament. In these various cases, hereditary factors will not of themselves bring disease. Impairment by the way of life remains the determining factor. "I get attacks of anxiety, I can't sleep, I have nervous troubles, it's a matter of one's 'climate of life'. I have a weak nervous system, which I've certainly inherited, but I might have set up home with a very very placid man, and had a different life, and now . . . I wouldn't have had these troubles."

Some people also show a tendency to restrict the role of heredity. The implicit question is: Is it really certain? "We don't really know why some people have abnormal children . . . there's heredity but . . . there are parents who are drunkards and others whose parents aren't drunkards, who are still abnormal."

Finally, according to some, hereditary diseases are very much rarer than those which are due to the way of life. "In big cities and certain industrial centres, people are on edge . . . it's legitimate to think that there's a higher incidence of mental disorders than elsewhere where there isn't this restlessness. There's heredity if you like, but it doesn't count for all that much . . . in the cities, you come across so many queer folk in the street you don't really notice them." We can see that although heredity may be for this man a notion which he knows and uses, it is not really integrated into his thinking or, more generally, into his view of things. He no sooner mentions the case of hereditary diseases than he abandons it to return to what is for him essential and gives him, as it gives many others, a firm basis for his view: the way of life as the cause of our illnesses.

To summarize, the individual does not carry his illness essentially within himself; on the contrary, everything in him resists the encroachments of the way of life which tends to start it off. Internal individual factors play a part in so far as he resists strongly or weakly in the face of attack, but their part appears to be a secondary one compared with

that of the way of life which constitutes the principal and active determinant of disease. The individual can only resist; his role, although
important, is a secondary and passive one. "I think the way of life is
more important than the actual physical aspect; I don't think the
human being is ill as a result of inner factors; it is external conditions
which end by making him ill. Nevertheless, there are predispositions
. . . of children who are born less healthy than others, but I think it's
much more the environment which creates diseases."

On the other hand, constitution, temperament and heredity are, in
regard to health, determining factors which are both indispensable and
sufficient. The order of importance is here reversed. Health comes first
and foremost from the individual. "Health is a very special factor, due
first of all to heredity and then to the way of life of each person."

Thus, if illness is identified unequivocally with the way of life, the
individual is conversely described wholly in terms of resistance to
disease and, in fact, in terms of health. Generally speaking, then, individual factors, with which we have here been concerned, are assimilated
to health.

The outcome of this analysis would appear to be that health and
disease must be conceived as the outcome of a struggle between individual equals health and way of life equals disease. In this struggle we
have the opposition of an *active* factor, the way of life, which, by its
incursions, leads to disease, and a *passive* factor (passive being here
synonymous with resistance), the perfect health of the individual (or
the perfectly healthy individual). The outcome of the conflict may be
either the victory of the individual, resulting in health and adjustment
to the way of life, or the invalid way of life with deterioration in
health.

The representation thus involves a double opposition. The opposition
between health and illness originates in and reflects the opposition
between the passive individual and his exacting way of life. There
does not seem to be much point in referring again to the selective nature
of the schema here developed. If there are other images behind the
enveloping images of a harmful way of life and a resistant individual,
they are not, as the case of medical progress or of hereditary diseases
shows, integrated into a structured conception.

We prefer to draw attention to two other aspects.

1. The rigidly stereotyped nature of the schema immediately strikes
one. The notions of way of life as a factor in illness and of diseases of

civilization are daily emphasized by the mass media, including the national newspapers and the popular medical press. All the features of stereotypes—frequency and uniformity of expression of content, and the strongly emotional accompanying charge—appear here, and we may well think that subjects are having recourse to a schema which is in daily circulation in society, which is always available to them and which requires neither effort nor original thought.

2. Schematically, such a picture is nevertheless characterized by coherence of content and an organizing role in relation to reality. The struggle between the two opposing elements takes account both of different states (health and illness) and of different stages (in the development of a disease), and also, in this very process, elaborates a view or interpretation of the relations between the individual and his environment. Health and illness are distinguished in terms of the opposition between the individual and his way of life.

2
Nature, Constraint and Society

We have shown that there is a coherent representation of the basis of health and illness. This idea, which reflects reality and gives it meaning, would appear to arise because of the attribution of a common significance to the various aspects of the way of life.

Way of life and its meanings

The analysis of the notion of way of life does not consist merely of showing how it works. We must also be concerned with its content, which is made up of distinct elements.

The way of life indicates the spatio-temporal framework of the individual, the space in which he lives and its characteristic features (density of population, atmosphere, etc.), the rhythm of life (time schedules, forms of stimulation) and also the reflections of these in everyday forms of behaviour (eating, activities, sleeping and relaxation, for example). It is therefore in large measure something external to the person, but it also provides the common meaning for all of the conduct of each. Consider the place occupied by work: its setting, its rhythm and its conditions. A person's way of life is determined by his occupation and is subject to the demands of his specific function in society.

Life in cities appears as both *unhealthy* and *constraining*. Its harmful effects are due to these two characteristics. Its effects are channelled through various media (food, air, noise, rhythm of life and so on), but all of them share these two characteristics. One of the two aspects sometimes predominates. The idea of "unhealthy" is more important in respect of food, constraint in respect of noise and everything connected with the rhythm of life. This difference is, however, less important than what is common to both.

Let us first examine the notion of *constraint*. It comprises the image of a way of life imposed upon one, of an urban situation as un-avoidable as the human situation itself. Man can neither escape from it nor, in the main, alter it. "You can't reorganize your life, you are in a certain situation, it is there; there's a doctor who tells me to leave my job. That's fine, and I say to him: 'You leave *your* job'. You'd have to change your whole life, it isn't possible."

Confronted with his way of life, the individual thus feels himself passive and powerless. Constraint excludes any possibility of escaping from harmful conditions of living. It is also impossible for him, in everyday life, to avoid any of the more specific attacks on his health. Thus polluted air and noise, both unhealthy, are described as being imposed on the individual. "The noise in the street, the fumes in the air and the dust, how do you think you can move in the direction of health if technology is attacking you every minute like that?"

Again, every particular aspect appears to the individual as a con-straint, an imperative or a restriction, a noose in which he feels himself strangled and a prisoner. "We lead a restricted life, in town you are always shut in . . . you cross a street, but it seems to me that you are still imprisoned in this same street."

Finally, constraint has its effects on conduct. The individual feels himself forced into certain kinds of behaviour with which he isn't satisfied or which seem quite wrong to him. The rhythm of life and time schedules are experienced as constraints which are reflected in the conduct and habits of everyone. As one of the subjects interviewed said: "You have to think of everything, you have to think about getting up, about catching the bus, about getting there in time, about your work . . . you're always thinking, and that in itself creates a kind of dis-equilibrium . . . you're in the street, you aren't free, you have to look out for red lights, you have to pay attention to this and that, which means you're constantly on the look-out, your body is never at rest, always on the alert."

In short, the relation between the individual and his way of life is an externally imposed relation. The individual does not have the im-pression that he is creating it or participating freely in it, or even that he can appreciably modify it; he simply *undergoes* it. This leads to antagonism and conflict. A journalist summarizes thus his view of the contemporary way of life: "Today, the environment influences man much more than man influences the environment . . ."

The way of life, the determining factor in illness, is experienced by the individual as something external to him; way of life and illness impose themselves upon him, attack him and constrain him without, as it seems to him, his having any part in anything beyond his relatively passive capacity for resistance and adjustment to conflict.

These constraints and attacks are, in fact, those of social life. It is society, people think, which finds expression in the way of life, imposing obligations and restrictions upon us. It is society which brings conflict. "Very often, in present-day society, you have to control your-self and this is sometimes quite distressing, for things you can't do anything about anyway . . . You have to give way, society constrains you."

Similarly, it is because of one's social function, one's position in society that one can't change one's life. "Our current way of life, it's difficult to change it. If you wanted, as an individual, to live in a more balanced manner, you would be professionally and socially destroyed and that's something which would prevent you from doing it."

Finally, it is society which, through the way of life, brings illness; at the same time, it is society which demands that the individual should be healthy. "Good health, I think that in the face of the life you lead today, and the nervous tension you have to maintain, it provides de-fensive reserves against attack of any kind, whether by illness or by the society in which you live. The individual with good health can rely on himself, so it's a factor which makes for assurance and confidence and that has enormous possibilities for the individual in society . . ."

This man expresses the double role of health in the individual–society conflict. First of all it provides resistance to illness, which is a product of society. It also provides the physical reserve necessary for the effort of social adjustment.

Therein lies the paradox of society: it demands from the individual what it refuses him. We see here a hint of a more complex relation between the two parties to the conflict, which will enrich our initial schema. Society in its double role replaces the way of life—as bringing disease and as requiring health. For the individual, health is both the potential for resistance and the means of solving the conflict. The essential opposition, however, remains—the idea of opposition is even strengthened—between health as a factor internal to the individual, and the external factor of society and the way of life, experienced as threatening. Health is entirely endogenous; what is exogenous comes to stand for illness.

Health and nature—the artificial and the unhealthy

The view according to which life in society is the main source of illness is not, of course, new. Rousseau expressed it in the following way:

> The great inequality in manner of living, the extreme idleness of some, and the excessive labour of others, the easiness of exciting and gratifying our sensual appetites, the too exquisite foods of the wealthy . . . the unwholesome food of the poor . . . all these, together with sitting up late, and excesses of every kind, immoderate transports of every passion, fatigue, mental exhaustion, the innumerable pains and anxieties inseparable from every condition of life, by which the mind of man is incessantly tormented; these are too fatal proofs that the greater part of our ills are of our own making, and that we might have avoided them nearly all by adhering to that simple, uniform and solitary manner of life which nature prescribed. . . . When we think of the good constitution of the savages, at least of those whom we have not ruined with our spirituous liquors, and reflect that they are troubled with hardly any disorders, save wounds and old age, we are tempted to believe that, in following the history of civil society, we shall be telling also that of human sickness.
>
> 1913, pp. 166-167

Rousseau himself only took up ideas which had been put forward a long time before. Without going back to the distant past, we know that the great navigators, beginning from the 16th century and continuing through the 17th and 18th centuries, on their return from their voyages, spread the myth of the noble savage, health and happy in a paradise-like state of nature. During the 19th century, the notion of the noble savage lost ground, but the idea that health had its source in the harmony of the individual with nature persisted. Jenner, for example, wrote: "Man has been overwhelmed by illness since the time he abandoned the path that nature had traced for him." (Quoted by Dubos, 1961, chapter 1.)

The belief is then that science will enable men, who have lost the conditions and the "instincts" of natural life, to rediscover the ways of health by precise knowledge. These indicate various ways in which nature and society are thought of as opposed, and we shall follow them up in our analysis of the notion of the *unhealthy* which, in association with the notion of constraint, characterizes the way of life.

The way of life is not only unhealthy, it is also "abnormal", "artificial" or "not natural" or "chemical"; similarly, the "healthy life", in opposition to the urban way of life, appears as "normal" and "natural". All these terms, indeed, seem to be more or less interchangeable, if not synonymous in use. "When you think of a healthy life . . . you think of a rhythm of life nearer to nature than the rhythm

of life imposed by the town." "Many people who work in towns live
in an abnormal way . . . country life is healthier." "For me, the life in
big towns is an abnormal life . . . as far as food is concerned, you don't
have a normal healthy, natural life . . . you don't have a normal
nervous or social life either . . ."

These pronouncements give an impression of verbalism. What is the
basis for the ubiquitous, almost inevitable, quality of the terms "natural–
artificial" and "healthy–unhealthy" in these statements? Certainly not
their precise meaning, but rather the extent of their evocative power.
Is it their rootedness in the culture which releases most people from the
need for any futile effort after precision? However that may be, the
healthy–unhealthy contrast functions as the norm for judging health
or illness. In it are condensed two series of ideas or images. (1) The
idea, sometimes vague but always implied, of "nature" and the
"natural"; the unhealthy designates the infringement of this natural
state. "The way of life is more natural in the country; we mustn't cut
ourselves off from nature, that seems to me disastrous." (2) This in-
fringing includes the notion of *heterogeneity*; in particular, it often involves
the introduction into "nature" of elements of a quite different kind.
To put it in more concrete terms, the way of life is unhealthy in the
first place because of the products which it creates or transforms, in
the second place because of the behaviour to which it gives rise. In
particular, there are food products which appear unhealthy because
their natural character and original composition have been altered.
The introduction of heterogeneous elements here should be interpreted
strictly; it refers to the presence of "chemical" elements, and suggests
pollution. "They say that the products of the earth are not so rich, are
not healthy perhaps because there are chemicals in them. To make
hens lay, they give them frightful things to eat . . . the eggs are unhealthy, harmful, indigestible."

But the composition of the food is not the only issue. What happens
to it is equally seen as "unhealthy" and makes it different from what
it originally was. In the last resort, it would appear that any kind of
interference or processing can come to be regarded as suspect. "In the
offices . . . all the secretaries have a packet of biscuits in the drawer . . .
and biscuits are an artificial product . . . and therefore not really fit
to eat."

Frequently, terms are used which imply complex and doubtful
manipulation. The product is forced, chopped about, faked. The

idea of deception is here implied: things are artificial or artificially transformed; they are less genuine. On the other hand, the healthy product is genuine and people insist on its origin; it comes, as they say, straight from the earth, straight from the animal. "Chemical remedies . . . are something manufactured from a product which is a synthesis or chemical reconstitution of natural products . . . and homeopathic remedies are the thing itself, extracted either from the animal or from the earth."

Another important aspect appears in the idea of a "forced" product; the disturbing of the temporal rhythm involved in the coming to maturity of a product is a typical technique for changing its "natural" character. "When I used to go on holiday to my grandparents in Auvergne, they had an old oven for baking bread, and when you made bread, you made enough for a fortnight, you spent a whole day making the dough rise, and then there were three hours in an oven heated by a wood fire. The baker makes his bread with oil-firing in a quarter of an hour . . . well, there's a kind of natural condition which we no longer observe . . . there's a time which it's natural to allow for the dough to rise and you have to have the necessary time to cook it."

We need not dwell upon the rather mythical nature of this contrast between the chemical and manufactured on the one hand and the natural on the other. Objectivity merges with irrationality and information with rumour. It is not our concern to separate truth from falsehood or act as judge or expert, but rather to understand the mechanism at work. Resistance to change can be seen clearly here; what might be called progress becomes regarded instead as pollution while it is thought that only a return to traditional country methods would enable us to obtain healthy products. "Now we are being told to grow vegetables as they used to be grown, without using chemicals, without forcing them, to get back to natural products."

Food is not the only thing in question; the *air* we breathe is also a natural product, denaturalized by the way of life, assailed by foreign elements, vitiated or polluted. "The air in Paris has been analysed and they found that factory fumes and exhaust fumes were seriously polluting the air, charging it with certain molecules which induced diseases of the blood and of the nerves and even a certain kind of cancer."

The individual thus feels himself to be attacked by the swallowing and breathing of these unnatural products released by the way of life.

He also feels that he is forced into behaviour of an essentially similar character; the way of life forces upon the individual behaviour which he considers unnatural and thereby abnormal and harmful, or else it prevents natural behaviour from taking place. "Natural acts have become complicated in modern life."

It is not so much separate products as the way of life in its entirety which is seen as denaturalizing, and thereby harmful. A taxi driver, particularly allergic to his way of life, describes it in the same terms as he would use for a polluted product. "I'm living in a closed box in this industrial life, this artificial life, this chemical life." The term "chemical life" expresses for him, better than any other term, the sense of incompatibility between his life and himself. Similarly, he sees himself as made abnormal, or denaturalized, by this state of affairs. "After midday, I'm already living on my nerves, I feel worn out and then I go on with my work until seven o'clock and at seven o'clock I'm no longer a normal man."

Another subject, a postmaster, uses the same expression. "I think that man, in spite of the advantages of progress, is ending up by becoming denaturalized."

We must now consider the reasons put forward to explain why the way of life is harmful to the individual and the values opposed to such a way of life. These may be divided into three categories.

1. First of all, there are frequent references to different and healthier ways of life.

References to the past "We always have to be running, life is more intensely active than before; formerly, you lived more calmly, more healthily, it seems to me."

References to life in the country Life in the country is referred to as "the ideal way of life for health", as natural, healthy and non-constraining, and is contrasted item by item with the urban life which is imposed upon us. The most important aspects concern the more relaxed rhythm of activities and the calmness associated with country life. Attention is also paid to the quality of the air and to the possibilities of physical exercise. There is finally the belief in the possibility of healthy food, different from that obtainable in towns.

Like life in the town, however, life in the country is conceived as a whole, all aspects reinforcing each other to produce an idyllic picture of a well balanced man in a healthy way of life, and of harmony rediscovered in nature. "I saw how people lived in the country . . . two

years ago, I went to Lozere . . . well, everybody's healthy . . . the food
is nothing much, people don't eat very well because they're very poor
down there . . . but their animals grow up in a normal way, first of all
because they couldn't think of buying chemical products, they would
be afraid . . . I think these people live more healthily, go to bed earlier,
don't have so many fumes in the air and take fewer stimulants . . . you
see people down there as strong as a rock . . ."

These references to other ways of life—this contrast between old-
rural-healthy and present-day-urban-unhealthy—may be interpreted
as attributing a contingent character to the present-day way of life; it
is only one way of life among others. Moreover, it represents a mutation
rather than a result of evolution, it is discontinuous with and at variance
with former ways of life. It therefore appears as the result of chance,
an anomaly of which the individual feels himself to be the victim.

2. We can now understand the significance of the second type of argument invoked; to the effect that the present-day way of life, which is a
denaturalized deviation from normal development, is not adapted to
man. This view is sometimes expressed in reference to the individual
case. "The imprisoned life one leads in Paris doesn't suit my temperament." It sometimes takes the form of a general pronouncement. "I
think the human machine isn't really made for this kind of life . . . in
general, towns are the kind of places to make people ill . . ."

According to these views, unhealthiness is not an intrinsic quality of
an object; a product or a kind of behaviour is unhealthy only because
it is unhealthy for the individual and in relation to the individual.
Again, to see in unhealthiness more than a quality of an object implies
a concern with the discordant relation between the object and the
person; they do not fit one another. Sometimes we also find an in-
sistence on the notion of harmfulness being relative to persons, their
needs and their peculiarities. What is unhealthy may be an individual
matter. We find it said, for example: "What I myself can't stand in
Paris is the noise, it seems to tire me; for others, it would be the air or
something else, but it's the noise that's bad for me."

From the same point of view, what is natural is not seen just as a
quality of an object but is thought of in a clearly anthropomorphic
way. What is natural is in fact what is thought to be suited to man
or to be like him. We might almost say that instead of man being
thought of as adapted to nature, it is nature which is thought of as
adapted to man. Thus, an office worker refers to herself as natural.

What is healthy then implies a degree of harmony between herself and certain fitting objects, equally natural. "I am quite natural, everybody is natural . . . and natural remedies work better with me than chemical things."

Conversely, in the conflict between the individual and an unhealthy object, there is a double discordance. Nature is twice transformed, in the object itself and equally, if not more so, in the individual affected. In short, it is man and his nature which are the measure of the healthy and the unhealthy. Again we find this contrast, which is basic in the representation between that which has the characteristics of the individual, that which is him or is concordant with him, and thereby healthy and natural, and that which is alien, discordant and unhealthy.

3. This interpretation is strengthened by an examination of the third group of ideas invoked, those involving constraint. Constraint functions, as we have indicated, to prevent anyone from escaping from the way of life and its onslaught. But in some cases, most frequently in relation to the rhythm of life or of activities, *constraint itself appears threatening;* the fast rhythm of life is unhealthy because and when it is imposed upon us. "To be forced always to keep up this rhythm, to hurry because you know you still have to do this and that and you're obliged . . . that's not normal and eventually you pay for it."

The same rhythm of activity, freely adopted by the individual, would lose much of its unhealthy quality. And we shall see that equilibrium, a superior form of health, is described as the possibility of accelerating one's rhythm of life at will, of "stepping oneself up", increasing one's efforts, or as the possibility of extreme physical exertion freely undertaken (see chapter 4). Several individual cases indicate, conversely, that the way of life is not in itself either healthy or unhealthy but that an unhealthy—or healthy—relation is established for each individual with the constraining aspect of the way of life and the tension which results therefrom. Thus, a young painter who realized that his urban way of life resulted entirely from his own choice refused to consider it as unhealthy. He said: "I actually prefer the town, I love the city atmosphere, I couldn't live anywhere but Paris. People often say that a town like Paris causes certain diseases, there are statistics showing this, apparently . . . I must say I don't agree with this; you can live in the city without being ill."

He found no difficulty in questioning the very general nature of the statistics and citing his own case in contrast. Thus, the individual who has been able to choose his way of life clearly and without constraint, remains even in the city in touch with a healthy life and with nature. "I believe that, with health . . . you must essentially go on being yourself and trying to know yourself as well as possible by examining yourself. You have to feel at home in whatever way of living . . . to say that people should be obliged to live in the country because it's nearer to nature, I think that just isn't so. Nature is first and foremost yourself, not something else. I think that even when you're in the underground, nature's there just as much as in any part of the country. Take me, for example, I don't need any holidays at all . . . to see a tree in the street is enough, and in the underground, to see people's heads . . . I find nature and life everywhere. There are things you have to find out yourself, you have to become aware of what you need and I think that always comes back to the same thing—to know yourself as well as you can . . . and I think that in this way man can very well live in the city."

Conversely, a Parisian housewife living in the country against her will says of her way of life that the calm, the absence of noise and stimulation, the regularity of her life, in short, all the elements of the healthy life have an adverse effect. She actually uses the very same expressions as the Parisian subjects; for her also the result is fatigue, malaise, nerves. "I was well enough when I lived in Paris, my nerves are worse here . . . I have difficulty in sleeping and when I go to Paris for a fortnight's holiday, I no longer have headaches and I can sleep. I'm bored and I think that has a lot to do with one's state of health; but you have to go where your husband's business takes him and there's nothing you can do about it. I find that, even though I lived a very active and stimulating life in Paris, I wouldn't feel any more tired living in Paris than living here and saying to myself: What on earth am I going to do?. I find this extremely regular life too quiet, altogether too quiet. In winter, when you no longer see a living soul in the street, well, this quiet gets me and makes me nervous."

In short, the way of life is unhealthy for the individual because it isn't made for him, but also because he is not made for it. One must inevitably be struck by the paradoxical aspect of such a view. When we look at the notions of what is unhealthy and artificial, we find that it is always the product of technology or of human activity which is felt to be the cause. Although it is identified with society, it nevertheless appears to the individual as something outside him, foreign to his nature and constraining. On the other hand, fundamental constraining factors like the natural rhythm of growth of a plant are identified with the notion of the healthy and anthropomorphically with man himself. If illness arises from a conflict between the individual and society, the unhealthy arises in the last resort from the antagonism perceived to exist between what is felt to be the nature of man and the form and product of his activities.

A world without illness, or, health as a constraint

The unhealthy, unnatural constraining society brings man illness. This is the common theme of our analyses, the thread which binds them together. We wished in some sense to test this notion by asking the question: Could a world without illness exist?

Few people believe that it could. It would imply a radical transformation of man. "It doesn't seem to me possible with human beings as they are today. I think it would be necessary to change the whole of human nature."

Such a transformation could only result from an unlimited power to plan society, a power which would completely control the life of the individual and, in so doing, would impose health upon him. "I wonder if it's possible . . . because you can't really control the individual completely, individuals just *have* personal instincts which you can't reduce, and which won't change; and we should all have to have the same way of living, the same way of thinking and the same way of feeding, which isn't easy to control. You would have to be subject to domination by something . . . Society would have to control everything."

Such a solution seems scarcely possible in its strictest sense, but for some people it represents the limiting point—absurd and dangerous—of present evolutionary processes. In this case, health is produced by society and is identified with society, and loses much of its value for the individual. Many of our subjects rejected this kind of solution or expressed doubts.

"The idea of a world in which you would try to foresee everything, and in which the whole of humanity would be as it were in a great cocoon rather horrifies me . . . this organized business . . . I don't think that conquests by man in this direction are desirable."

Health, by a further paradox, thus ceases to be natural. "You can't imagine it, it would be contrary to nature . . . it would no longer be natural health . . . I wouldn't want to see it, it's so abnormal."

The "nature" of man is again in question; it would then be threatened by health just as in the world of today it is threatened by disease. The "world without illness" endangers the psychological and personal integrity of man. "It seems to me to presuppose an even more complete mechanization of men and this I entirely disapprove of; we are falling at this very moment into that kind of negation of humanity, in this artificial kind of humanity."

Indeed, man's physical integrity itself is seen as threatened, since man would have lost his capacity for physical resistance which today is the source of health. "The human machine is what it is because it has been able to train itself to resist certain diseases and to defend itself. If it lost the habit of struggling against external agents . . . it rather strikes me that it would degenerate . . . in this state, which would in fact be an abnormal state, with the slightest infection . . . suddenly, it's all over, you just die . . ."

Thus we find illness and death again, this time on the side of nature and therefore on the side of the individual; death indeed is qualified as a natural necessity, bound up with the preservation of the species. "Deaths are necessary . . . It's the law of nature, you have to disappear and make room for others."

Illness, on the other hand, is seen as the expression of an individual need, the possibility of evasion. "I won't say that illness is a *need* that people have, but it is often a means of flight in relation to society and the duties one is shirking, and I think there will always be people who are ill. Even if you could manage to suppress diseases physically, they would have psychological causes."

Illness represents freedom in the face of the alienating society. "Finally, there is the factor of chance . . . the sense of freedom, and then the aspect involved in overcoming illness, all that would vanish if illness disappeared."

The importance attached to social constraint is so great that it can actually reverse the framework of associations which we have seen emerging, while the very same terms are retained. The conflict then becomes one between a society constraining by its health and the individual whose nature now includes and finds expression in illness.

The representation is thus built up by the simultaneous manipulation

of a series of opposing terms: internal and external, healthy and unhealthy, natural and unnatural, the individual and society. Our analysis
of constraint, of the unhealthy, of the natural has enabled us to
develop a little the original contrast between health and illness, between
the individual and his way of life, and has indicated how these contrasts
recur and are delimited in the series of other contrasts.

In this way we arrive at the view that it is not so much the actual
content of each notion that counts—none of them being wholly unambiguous—as the contrasts involved. The content may vary. An
object, i.e. a way of life, is not wholly either healthy or unhealthy, either
natural or artificial. The bipolar classification, however, remains and
serves to establish the differentiation between health and illness.

There are two terms which seem to be fundamental: the individual
and society. The other contrasts reduce, in effect, to this one, and even
when the classificatory scheme is inverted (cf. the analysis of the "world
without illness", p. 38), the overriding factor of the constraint of society
on the individual remains constant. In fact, it is social constraint which
is at the root of what is unhealthy, and thus at the root of illness. We
can now better understand the significance of our initial proposition
(see p. 28) to the effect that a social definition of the genesis of health
and illness comes about through the attribution to the various different
factors in the way of life of a common significance. It is the constraint
imposed by society which canalizes the adverse effects of the way of life.

3
Mechanisms and Usage

Two points remain obscure in relation to the genesis of health and illness. (1) How do people view the releasing of illness and the mechanisms involved? (2) How is the model which we have found most appropriate—of society as the producer of disease, opposed to the individual defined in terms of his health—used by our subjects? What contribution does it make towards the constitution of reality as the individual perceives it?

A mechanism: toxicity

Toxicity, strictly speaking, refers to the ingestion or forced retention by the organism of harmful substances. As we use it here, the term refers to the ingestion of unhealthy substances which results from the way of life. Toxicity, according to this view, is the releasing mechanism of illness characteristic of and specific to a particular representation.

A number of writers have noted the importance of the idea of toxicity (or poison) in notions of illness, and have emphasized its ancient roots and its universality. Green (1961), in a study of the violent campaign of opposition encountered by attempts to fluoridize water supplies in the United States analyses at length the argument centred on poisoning and the danger of toxicity invoked by all the opponents of fluoridation. In an account rather similar to the present one, he emphasizes the location of the specific notion of toxicity in a wider ideological context, and shows how this argument is related to a view of society as alienating and as imposing upon the individual among other measures, measures harmful to his physical integrity. Green, however, considers the toxicity argument as secondary and in some measure as concealing the basic reasons for the opposition (the alienation of man by society). Our view, on the other hand, is that the toxicity theme should be taken literally as well as metaphorically. In our own data, the idea of toxicity expresses the threat of the way of life and its effect on the individual. It is the concept essential for relating the two sides of the conflict.

The notion of toxicity appears frequently in our data. It can be compared in this respect to invasion by germs (although the two ideas are not strictly equivalent: germs are an agent while toxicity is a process). In spite of the spreading of the idea of germs, through instruction in schools, this notion is referred to by only half of our subjects, while two-thirds refer to toxicity.

Three aspects can be discerned in the ways in which the notion is used.

1. Because of the general and highly variable form of this notion, everything or almost everything in the way of life can appear toxic; for instance food, tobacco, contaminated air, even noise or excessive activity. Toxicity due to food or alcohol is obviously of particular importance. Toxicity is produced first and foremost by over-eating. "I think we eat too much, too much food is surely harmful; I suppose you accumulate too many calories, you get full of poisons . . . and they aren't eliminated."

Naturally, chemical products, foreign bodies *par excellence*, are especially important. "You absorb a formidable quantity of chemical products which are harmful to individuals . . . you can quite easily absorb a small quantity of toxic products . . . you use these products in very small amounts as traces, but this doesn't mean that the continued absorption of these substances doesn't slowly but surely kill you . . ."

Again, the process of absorbing toxins refers not only to the introduction of harmful substances into the organism, but also to their forced retention. As soon as the idea of a toxin appears, the way of life is also brought into the picture. Thus, elimination is prevented by the fact that our way of life does not allow us sufficient exercise. "The city dweller doesn't undertake physical exercise, he doesn't burn up all he eats, he accumulates toxins in his blood in addition to the chemical products and impurities he breathes."

The atmosphere can be toxic as well as food, of course. "When I pass a truck, I feel that I'm breathing in poison, and I'm disgusted— but this sense of smell is a defence, because it's poisonous, I feel it. I'm being poisoned."

It is more interesting and less commonplace to find the same kind of use of the idea of toxicity in relation to activity or to noise. Here again we have the idea of poison and of the continued and repeated nature of the threat. "We have noise coming from the street all day, you don't notice it any more because you're used to hearing it. All your senses are adapted to it, it's like a poison that you take every day, you don't taste it any more, but it's harmful just the same, every drop adds to the rest."

Even when we have to deal with less physical things than alimentary or respiratory toxicity, the use of the metaphors and language of toxicity enables us to specify the process. The triggering of an illness by nervous exhaustion or emotional disturbance—and here we may apply psychosomatic theories—may be thought of in terms of this model, even though the term "toxicity" is not used. Emotions and stimulation may appear as so many poisons, secretions of the way of life which threaten us just like chemical products and just as continuously. "The frightening life we lead, all the propaganda around us, the advertisements, everything you see, all the things they tell us . . . the fact of always being ready to hear more or less catastrophic news of things that have happened more or less anywhere, the nervous tension we live in . . . everybody lives with ideas of violence, and so this maintains our nervous state, our state of tension, this keeps us always on the stretch."

2. Toxicity is thought of as a slow and repeated process, the effects of which can only be fully obvious in the long term. While attack by germs is seen as a crude process of the "all or nothing" kind, toxicity is cumulative; every threat is, in itself, insufficient to be really harmful, but the effects add up. Things happen as if the foreign character of the product, or of any other factor in the way of life, became more appreciable as time passes. The relation between the individual and the toxic factor becomes, in consequence, progressively more unhealthy. "Certainly, there must be something in the air we breathe which isn't perhaps dangerous at the moment, but in the long run . . . it triggers things off."

3. Finally, we have its "dynamic" character. Toxicity is the mechanism which particularly expresses the conflict involved in the encounter between the unhealthy way of life and the threatened individual. Firstly it may be viewed as a process extending over time. By virtue of its quality of slow accumulation its full effects only appear in the long term; decline in health is an intermediate stage in the process of the "release" of the illness. Secondly, both poles of the contrast are brought together by the concept of toxicity, for it implies internalization of the

unhealthy. Comparison with the notion of germs helps us here, since germs are themselves the threatening agent, while in toxicity the threatening entity and the individual threatened come together.

The model of the genesis of health and illness is completed by the notion of toxicity. The many-sided and repeated threat of the way of life is here clearly considered as a concrete reality. It takes the definite form of the obligatory assimilation by the individual of what is foreign and harmful to him.

We do, nevertheless, sometimes see the reciprocal process: *accommodation*. One becomes "poisoned" by the repeated attacks of the way of life; but one can also adapt to them. "I think that the organism must adjust, or else we'd all be dead."

In this case, the effects do not accumulate, but tail off, and become progressively less harmful to the individual. The threatening foreign element becomes progressively more acceptable to the individual; the relation thus gradually loses its unhealthy character. There remains, however, an unresolved problem: Why should there be cases both of toxicity and adaptation?

It is difficult to provide an answer to this question, which is certainly posed in rather specific terms. However, the view of one man suggests a possible hypothesis: the individual's adaptation becomes more probable, the greater his capacity for organic defence, and the more resistant he is. "There is also a processs of adaptation; gradually, the body becomes resistant . . . the extent depends on the individual . . . I think it's connected with the individual's defensive resources—for some people, the body defends itself very well, for others, not at all."

Perception and anticipation

How does the individual become aware of the threat to his way of life? What are the psychological processes involved? We may distinguish two aspects, one involving perceptual mechanisms, the other involving what may be called predictive or anticipatory aspects. The perceptual aspect is primary and essential; the way of life is perceived through a wide variety of sensory indices (sight, sound, taste and smell). Consider the statement of one subject, whose views we have quoted before. "To hear the noise in the street, to feel the bad smells, this all attacks me as soon as I go out in the morning, I feel there are hundreds of things threatening my health, smells, when I pass a truck, I feel that I am breathing in poison, but this sense of smell is a defence, because I feel I'm being poisoned."

There are many examples which demonstrate the importance of sensory information in our awareness of our way of life. In them the individual is directly aware of harmfulness. Through them, the way of life appears as unequivocally unhealthy. These perceptions have, in fact, the character of immediate evidence; what is experienced in sensory terms really is a threat and conflict. "Noise and the poison that affects the air we breathe is a terrible thing. I feel that my organism rebels, it shocks me and makes me nervous."

In short, the harmful nature of the way of life is not, for the individual, an *a posteriori* deduction, or the result of an intellectual reconstruction. It is the object of a perception. The way of life is seen in sensory terms as harmful. Some of our subjects maintained that the external object itself was a causative factor; thus we may note, for example, reference to the decline in the quality and taste of food.[1] "Formerly, if you only ate a carrot, the carrot did something for you, but today, if you eat a carrot, it has no taste, it gives you less vitamins than before . . . Nowadays, they fatten chickens with ever so much starch; well, this chicken doesn't taste as good as a chicken which runs about and is brought up on corn. And so, to my way of thinking, it's flesh can't give you as many calories."

Sometimes, on the contrary, the people interviewed stressed the immediate perception of an inner effect. Organic images, precise and suggestive in their very incongruity, appear. They indicate that the body is very much involved.

"The air in Paris doesn't agree with me at all, in Paris I always have a feeling of heaviness, a feeling that my thinking is slowed down, that my blood is heavy." "I can't stand noise . . . I feel my nerves tying themselves in knots, that's just what I feel—tying themselves in knots." "In the country, I can eat anything . . . in Paris, I try an egg . . . I feel as if someone had stuck a dagger in my liver." "I live partly on my nerves, my nerves help me a lot, but with the pace in Paris, you can't leave it all to them . . . and I feel them giving way, so they don't help any more—in fact, they are a nuisance."

At the same time, some subjects refer to the healthy way of life

---

[1] Taste and smell seem to be special senses, in the sense that they are dependable. The role of sight seems more doubtful; some subjects, for example, emphasize that food which looks nice may sometimes be deceptive.

and its positive relation to the person and its beneficial effect on the organism. The sensory perceptions of what is healthy and what is unhealthy indicate that a schematic model of things, of the way of life as a cause of illness for us, appears here as the direct perceptual reflection of reality, with the status of objective evidence. Every perceptible index has the significance of an unequivocal sign of illness or of health. We can say more: illness and health "in embryo" find objective representation in the way of life. In particular, faced with the unhealthy way of life, from his first feeling of being threatened, and often independently of any clear effect on his condition, the individual experiences the attempted intrusion of illness as the attempted intrusion of an object. He perceives its presence in the way of life, even when there are no manifestations of it in himself.

These objective perceptions may appear to some extent unexpected, in so far as we have interpreted the idea of the unhealthy as expressing the relation to the individual rather than as an intrinsic quality of the way of life. The two aspects are, however, complementary; the way of life is unhealthy for the individual in relation to him, but the awareness of the conflict as something experienced tends to give the unhealthy a concrete reality external to the individual.

To the actual perception of the unhealthy, however, is added a classificatory judgement which enables the individual to orient himself simultaneously to the everyday reality of the way of life and to the universe of health and illness. Thus the model, reflecting reality, becomes an instrument in terms of which phenomena can be categorized: one way of life is distinguished from another and this distinction appears in the form of a classificatory scheme for the states themselves: an unhealthy way of life and illness, a healthy life and health each constitute a unique entity for the individual. Judgements to the effect that the urban way of life provokes illness do not then simply represent a perception of reality but are used in an anticipatory way to predict one's own condition and that of others.

Paradoxically, in fact, the individual sees illness as residing in the way of life, as caused by it, better and with more evidence than he can see it in himself. The way of life is, no doubt, pathogenic, but, in fact, objective verifications of attack by the occurrence of an illness are rare and their meaning is not always clear. When he thinks about his own condition, the individual is daily aware, as we have seen, of vague states of fatigue, nervousness and malaise. He experiences them as the direct effect of the conflict between himself and the way of life, but he only rarely sees the beginning of a specific illness as a direct and obvious consequence of the effect of the way of life. We are forced to the un-expected conclusion that illness is "perceived" in the way of life and in the conflict which it engenders and is predicted by the individual as the logical consequence of the present state of affairs and frequently without reference to any actual occurrence.

It is just as if, on the basis of his conviction, based on his immediate sensory experience of the pathogenic nature of the way of life and the uncertainty or ambiguity of his own states, caught between the evidence of the omnipresence of illness in the way of life and the relative rarity of objective proofs provided by actual illnesses, the individual resolves his dilemma by anticipation. Since illness is, in any case, in embryo in the way of life, he feels entitled to anticipate it and to foresee it in him-self. His awareness of threat convinces him that illness, although not immediately obvious, is nevertheless there and will, or may, show itself at a later stage. Expressions to this effect are common. "In the long run, all these little discomforts become illness." "People who are exhausted end by getting illnesses such as stomach ulcers." "In the long run, it ends by setting things off."

Conversely, when the subjects were asked about an actual illness, they attributed its origin to the way of life, this time retrospectively.

We can now better appreciate the importance of the notion of toxicity. It is the concept logically necessary to relate the present per-ceptions of the individual—the unhealthiness of the way of life and his own state of fatigue or malaise—to the anticipated illness. Illness is already potentially there from the time of the first ingestion of anything unhealthy and it is by a process of gradual accumulation of toxins that the process continues to its conclusion; resistance slowly declines and, correspondingly, the intermediate state gives way to acknow-ledged illness.

Some reflections on the genesis of health and illness

In terms of our analysis, illness is in origin a "thing" produced by the way of life and, in the last resort, by society. It arises from the material-ization and accumulation of unhealthy elements which threaten the individual. But the individual has a certain margin of freedom to respond to this "thing" with the resistance of health. The conflict between these two factors is thus manifested in actual states of health and illness. If we recall the classic theories of the exogenous or endogenous origin of illness, we shall see that the notions to which we have referred attribute illness primarily to an exogenous origin. Illness comes from the way of life and from society. The process of development is, however, more complex; illness depends on both the individual and the way of life, each playing a part. The case of health, on the other hand, is simpler: it is entirely contained within the individual and never lies outside him. While illness appears as the result of a process of interaction or conflict, health is immediately given. To put it in an extreme form, it might be said that health has no genesis while illness has.

We should also observe the convergence between scientific theories and notions current among the public. For science too, understanding the phenomenon of illness means trying to clarify the interaction between internal and external factors. Professor Maurice Lamy writes: "After due consideration, it must be acknowledged that there are really three kinds of illness. In the first, the 'threat' is crucial and defence— one might say predisposition—is of no significance. In the second kind, the individual constitution is the crucial factor. The final kind of illness includes those illnesses which are due to the combined influence of both factors." (1964, p. 46.)

Similarly, the idea of variations in illnesses associated with a particular way of life and era seems to have a good scientific basis—Charles Nicolle called a famous work "The Birth, Life and Death of Infectious Diseases". More generally, too, the conceptions of our subjects may be related to the major historical current of thought which, up to the 19th century, saw in health or illness the result of a harmony—or lack of harmony—between man and his environment.

The ideas to which we have directed attention, however, seem to be characterized by the fact that the relations between man and his environment are conceived wholly in terms of conflict. The exogenous or external is equated unreservedly with illness and the endogenous or internal with health. The opposition of these two sets of factors to one another seems to be complete. Any interaction or adjustment in the relations between the individual and his environment seem lacking in such a view. Any kind of coexistence other than an armed one, between the individual and the pathogenic factors, appears impossible.

The implications of this view for the picture of the organism which emerges should be clear. The organism becomes defined essentially in terms of its capacity for resistance, like a more or less solid substance, rather than by the adaptability or integrated nature of its functioning. Likewise, such a notion includes the relation between health and illness, defined entirely in terms of conflict. These then appear as two quite different aspects of reality. There is no sign of a conception which would assume a kind of common ground between them, seeing them as different expressions of a single vital principle, on one continuum. Health and illness appear as two phenomena without any common quality in terms of which the conflict could be resolved.

During our whole analysis we have emphasized the rather schematic nature of the conceptions involved. The model which emerges is that of a series of conflicts the heart of which lies in the two-fold opposition of health and illness, of individual and society. Before continuing our analysis, let us consider for a moment the function of this model. Such a definition, explaining health and illness by an interpretation of the relations of the individual and society, would appear to represent a double defence of the individual—against society and against illness. The individual distinguishes himself from the threatening society and by doing so affirms his non-participation in illness. Illness comes from the way of life, from society. Defence, in this sense, is also a form of accusation. From this point of view we can understand more fully the significance of the schematic dualism of the system and the rigidity of the contrasts. The fundamental differentiation between self as source of health and other as bringer of illness finds expression in the contrasts between individual and society, between healthy and unhealthy and between natural and artificial.

Stoetzel (1960) has advanced the hypothesis that, through the diffusion of psychosomatic theories, our society may return, after the guilt-free germ theories, to a self-blaming conception of illness in which the individual feels himself responsible for his illness because of the mental conflicts which have induced it. Again, in a point of view like Balint's, the idea of the participation of the individual in the genesis of his illness finds particularly clear expression; every individual is characterized by a "basic fault . . . involving in varying degrees both his mind and his body" (1957, chapter 19). Clinical diseases would then be symptoms or exacerbations of a basic defect in a particular situation.

The penetration of such ideas concerning the possible psychogenesis of diseases indeed appears undeniable; we have seen the importance

c

which our subjects attach to states of conflict and nervous tension. The intermediate state is a mental state as much as a physical one and is known to lead to or to facilitate the appearance of an illness. Again, the individual's resistance is sometimes said to be a nervous as well as a physical resistance. The overall meaning of the definition, however, would appear to lie in the refusal to assume responsibility in respect of the actual appearance of the illness. Whatever the importance of mental states in its development, the responsibility for the actual beginning of the illness belongs to the way of life. It is, after all, the way of life which provides the harmful stimulation and causes of nervous tension and anxiety. The individual feels and affirms himself to be infinitely more threatened than guilty. (We shall have to qualify these interpretations when we come to study the patient and his behaviour. Guilt may exist *in* illness but it is not, at least consciously, guilt *because of* illness.)

On the other hand, the individual would appear to feel himself responsible for his health because, good or bad, it defines him. We suggest the hypothesis that, similarly, the individual feels guilty for having, in the conflict, allowed his health to be impaired or undermined, not for having caught an illness but for having lost his health.

Part 2

4
Health and Illnesses

While health and illness have so far appeared as unitary and clearly defined entities, the health of the individual being opposed to the illness of the way of life, the analysis of individual experience will force us to abandon this over-simplified picture and this deceptively clear-cut opposition. In fact, we find more than one kind of health and illness in people's experience and in everyday concepts. Health and illness are experienced as complex entities rather than as simple unities.

Thus, health can be experienced in various ways; it can be felt in a purely negative sense, and also as a positive state. It may be simply an *absence*—the absence of illness or the unawareness of the body, the "organic silence" of which Leriche spoke. In this case, it is barely a conscious phenomenon, barely a specific experience. One is said not to think of one's health and not to notice it until one has lost it. Thus, one subject said: "Health is basically a rather negative thing; as long as it isn't affected you don't realise that you are enjoying good health." He also made a more positive statement: "When you are in good health, you don't think about it, you think of other things."

At the same time, however, and indeed sometimes by the same people, health is experienced quite positively as a *presence* of which one is fully aware because of one's feeling of freedom and of bodily and functional well-being, or of resistance and physical robustness. "It is to feel in good form, happy, content, with a good appetite, sleeping well, wanting to be up and doing; it's to feel well and strong, that's what good health is."

As for illness, that appears both multiple and fractionated. The very phenomenon of illness appears multiple: illness is not viewed as a single entity, but illnesses appear in many forms. "Illness, 'illness' as such doesn't exist; there are many different illnesses, there are all sorts."

The diversity of illnesses referred to by the subjects interviewed is in this respect significant. They describe illnesses which they have had themselves or have seen in other people and illnesses which they know or fear. Their variety reflects the many sidedness of illness. Four groups of illnesses can be distinguished.

1. Illnesses which are or have been fatal and which are regarded as the principal scourges of the present or immediately preceding age.

2. Conversely, "common" illnesses like colds or 'flu' (which in respect of frequency come immediately after cancer and tuberculosis).

3. Childhood illnesses.

4. Illnesses which are in general trying for the individual because of their chronic or painful nature.

These illnesses thus vary in significance; they are regarded as fatal or crucial, or as quite trivial occurrences. Everyone, therefore, has only a partial experience of illness; each of us has experienced only one or a few illnesses which seem to the one concerned to be "particular" with respect to the totality of possible experiences of illness.

It is difficult to reconstitute illness from this fractionated experience. "Basically, I only know about two illnesses—I had pleurisy when I was fifteen, but that didn't cause me any pain, and then I've had stomach pains; that's my experience of illness—one of an illness with pain and one of an illness without pain."

Moreover, health and illness do not cover the whole field of individual experience; the state which some people find commonest is the *intermediate state* between health and illness. "There are all the little troubles, the little discomforts you have more or less all the year round—headaches, after-effects of alcohol, indigestion, fatigue. I don't think of these as illnesses; you aren't ill, but you aren't in good health either."

Finally, states are described which combine health and illness. In a way, one can be ill while healthy and enjoy good health while ill. Thus, some disorders do not impair one's health in the same way as a sudden illness, and a *status quo* is established. "I've had a stomach ulcer for ten years, but as long as I watch my diet it doesn't prevent me from enjoying good health."

Conversely, an illness can include a certain kind of good health. "During my pleurisy, I had good health, basically, I wasn't tired since I stayed in bed, I might almost say that I was in excellent shape."

A process of classification, however, is applied to this multiplicity, which both reflects it and imposes order upon it. The fluid data of experience are assigned to categories which result from a kind of spontaneous conceptualizing, and are ordered in terms of organizing schemata. A classification of states begins to emerge; forms of health and types of illness begin to be distinguished.

Health and its forms

The concept of health, in principle, is of little concern to the doctor; from a practical point of view only illness counts. The theoretical importance of what constitutes normality, however, cannot be denied. During the past few decades, psychiatrists, sociologists and psychologists have been especially concerned with the questions of psychological normality and mental health. A considerable number of definitions have here been attempted (see, for example, Jahoda 1953; Kubie 1954; Redlich 1957). In general, these have involved three kinds of criteria.

Absence of illness, which is frequently referred to, is generally re-garded as an inadequate criterion which takes account only of a necessary but insufficient minimum. Statistical criteria are also questioned, as is indicated by Kubie's formulation that "health is a state which is rare and yet not pathological". Attempts are also often made to identify health with positive symptoms or achievements. Emphasis is here placed on the fact that a symptom cannot be isolated from the whole individual, and that his achievement must be evaluated by reference to his position in the physical and social environment. The difficulty of evaluating and defining health is not thereby lessened.

Some writers have insisted that it may be futile to try to treat health as a single concept. Canguilhem (1950) indicates that there is both a descriptive and a normative concept of health. More recently, Vala-brega (1962) states that it is more accurate to speak of "healths" than of "health".

The examination of our data reveals a similar pluralistic conception of health. The representation includes not one health but "healths". The content of these "healths" can be ordered along three dimensions. Each of these can be thought of as a particular type, and we have named these types respectively, *health-in-a-vacuum*, *reserve of health* and *equilibrium*. Equilibrium is the one to which reference is most frequently made, but the different types occur together in subjects' remarks, each one having its own function. The analysis of each type, of the relations between them and of their part in the social representation, will allow us to grasp the differences between them and enable us to establish a hierarchy of types of health.

We have already mentioned the limited nature, in some cases, of actual experience of health. It is something of which one is simply not aware. But it may also be absent in the sense of being regarded as a phenomenon which can only be defined in terms of *lack*. What we have termed *health-in-a-vacuum* is simply *the absence of illness*. "Health is strictly speaking not something positive, it's simply not being ill."

Other people insist further that *lack of awareness of the body* is correlated with the absence of illness. "The fact of not having a body, so to speak, if it doesn't bother you in any way, health is basically an absence, it isn't anything positive, it's rather a negative thing."

More generally, health might be said to be when nothing is happening, the neutral ground against which illness, the happening, appears or may appear. As such, it is an absence of events. "Health is in short to live without noticing that time is passing; I think that if one day I wake up and I'm seventy, and I've lived like that, then I'll say that that's good health . . . in short, it will have been life without incidents."

Health is here reduced to a matter of fact, without psychological implications, and the concept refers simply to a negation of illness. The relation between health and illness is asymmetrical—illness is the only point of reference, the only experience, the only incident. Health, which is the negative pole, only reveals itself and assumes importance in consequence of the attack of illness which destroys it.

In contrast to the neutral state of health-in-a-vacuum, a second type of health can be observed which we have called "reserve of health", a term used by several of our subjects which seems an admirable summary and expression of the notions considered here. Its particular characteristic lies in its being a capital asset rather than a state. In the case of health-in-a-vacuum, one *is* in good health because one is not ill, but one *has* good health because of one's reserve of health. This capital asset has two main aspects: physical robustness or strength on the one hand and a certain potential for resistance to attacks, fatigue and illness on the other. "I've always had a sturdy constitution, a reserve of robust health; I think I am pretty resistant and not at all one of those with weak and precarious health."

While health-in-a-vacuum is something quite independent of the person, something impersonal, the *reserve of health* appears as an organic-biological characteristic of the individual as such. It is a part of each of us. A more detailed analysis will clarify its particular meaning.

We must first insist upon its physical basis; it is associated with notions of constitution and temperament, and some people regard it as congenital. "As far as I'm concerned, I've got excellent health, I was born with excellent health."

As such, it can have degrees; everyone is not born with the same reserve of health. It may be good, less good or poor, and may also vary according to the kind of life the individual leads; one may build up one's reserve of health, or break into it. This capital asset of vitality and defence may increase or dissipate in the course of time, like all capital. "I see people as much as ten years younger than me who already have white hair because they have passed the whole of their lives shut up in offices or little rooms. Certainly I attribute my capital health to the fact that I've lived more in the open air."

Childhood is a period especially favourable for developing a good reserve of health. "In a child, I think you have to get them to build up their strength when they are young. Perhaps it's an odd kind of theory, but I think that what's acquired when you are a child is never lost . . . it's always a good basis."

The reserve of health may vary, and may increase or decrease, but it *is*; it exists in a permanent sort of way. The individual will keep a certain reserve of health during his life, even though it be breached and attenuated by too exacting a life or attacked by age or illness. The following case is an extreme example of this kind of thing. "My father, who had excellent health, nevertheless had a very serious illness from which he died at the age of 72, but he had excellent health all the same, that was just chance."

In fact, we find in the analysis of the reserve of health all the features which characterize health conceived as a capacity for resistance to disease. The individual qualities (see chapter 1) which oppose illness and the attacks of the way of life become organized and clarified in the idea of a reserve of health particular to each individual.

But the reserve of health does not consist only of resistance to illness; it also appears as the "substructure" of the other types of health. It does not exclude either health or illness, but supports them equally in the proper sense of the term. This arises from its very nature. It is the reserve of defence from which everyone draws the possibility of reaction against illness. "I've had a whole heap of worries, you can just about cope with them when you have a good reserve of health, I mean healthy tissue and healthy bones."

The reserve of health thus represents, in this sense, an invariant which exists with both health and illness, which continues through the multiplicity of experienced states and which thereby allows a certain personal control of these states. It is because of this quality of positive but underlying reality that it rarely appears on the first level of personal experience of the individual. It is generally a reality which is deduced from more concrete experience of equilibrium or of illness, expressed by reference to the latter. "When I was ill, many people would have been very much reduced by it . . . I held out; I concluded that I owed it to my reserve of health."

One's reserve of health is often evaluated by comparison with other people. "When I see people around me, always tired, I tell myself that at any rate I've got good health."

Equilibrium, on the other hand, both in its presence and in its absence, represents an autonomous experience; one feels that one has equilibrium, or that one has lost it. There is no need for any comparison with others, and no need to refer to anything outside oneself in order to know. Equilibrium is "something there", an immediate personal experience. "When I am enjoying good health, I feel well, there's a sense of equilibrium when I feel that everything is going well, and difficulties appear quite insignificant." The same person also says: "When things aren't going right, I have more minor ailments . . . especially nervous ones, and I say to myself: 'Here . . . my equilibrium's upset'."

It is sometimes called "real" health; it is the superior form of health, good health in its highest sense, the realization in experience of the possibilities of the reserve of health, contrasted with the negative and inferior form regarded as health-in-a-vacuum. "There is not being ill . . . but there is also real health, when the body functions like a well-oiled machine, without having to be looked after . . . and there's also having sparkling eyes, a good colour, to feel at ease when you meet up with friends, and not to be all on edge."

Sometimes people wish for an "equilibrium medicine" promoting such a state. "Doctors look after you when you're ill, and so you don't get ill, but nobody looks after you from the point of view of good health and equilibrium." Moreover, equilibrium is not, like the reserve of health, something the continuity or permanence of which is asserted;

it either is or is not. Similarly, there are no degrees about it, no semi-equilibrium; at least, there are no references to such. Equilibrium is all or nothing.

From the preceding remarks, it would appear that we can regard the notion of equilibrium as a norm. Health-in-a-vacuum is only a fact, the reserve of health is a value, as is indeed indicated by the use of the term "reserve" with its associations of capital. Equilibrium also is a value, a state which one would like to attain or keep, or even a norm, and an individual norm at that; whether he feels himself to be in equilibrium or not, the individual judges his present state and the direction in which he is going by reference to himself. This perfectly "normal" state is in fact considered to be rare; it corresponds rather to a normative judgement than to a statistically predominating state of affairs. "People who are in perfect health, as you ought to be, well, I think you can see them now. But people who are really in equilibrium, they're very rare."

The very term "equilibrium" provokes comment. One is impressed by the relative frequency with which it is used and by the fact that it may be used as a noun or as an adjective, while there is also a corresponding verbal form. Thus the term has a wide variety of applications. It certainly indicates in the first place the state of the individual, that is his physical, nervous or indeed total or complete equilibrium. But it also refers to the person as such, described as a "person in equilibrium", and to the "equilibrium of his life". To reach equilibrium, a man attempts to balance his life. Just as the notion of "unhealthy" summarizes and expresses the experience of the way of life, the term "equilibrium", whether referring to act or state, as determinant and as resultant, serves to describe and express a whole area of individual experience. It serves, in a way, as a distillation of the language of health.

The notion and its usage, however, remain confused and poorly defined. People mention a number of things which *constitute* equilibrium, but no attempt is made to analyse in precisely what respect they constitute a state of equilibrium. For example: "Equilibrium is to feel happy, strong, at ease." If the experience seems clear enough, the choice of the term "equilibrium" to indicate it remains obscure. This does not appear, however, to be an obstacle to grasping the value overtones of the term; and in any case, its descriptive use may be not the most important. In his study of the social representation of psychoanalysis, Moscovici (1961, pp. 157–158) attributes to the term "complex" a two-fold function in communication which is descriptive and informative on the one hand and symbolic on the other. In the latter case, the term "complex" serves to indicate what one is talking about, to locate one in the field of psychoanalysis. It allows communication beyond the limits of precise understanding. Equilibrium would appear to have a similar function; despite, or because of, the relative absence of precise meaning, a kind of agreement becomes established between discussants on the basis of repeated use of the same terms, on a wide range of implicit meaning. Just by reference to equilibrium, personal aspirations and the specific and as it were indescribable quality of experience are relatively clearly communicated. Beyond merely indicating a state or symptoms, equilibrium is the key which opens the world of health, the symbol which transports us there.

Concretely, equilibrium comprises the following themes: physical well-being, plenty of physical resources; absence of fatigue; psychological well-being and evenness of temper; freedom of movement and effectiveness in action; good relations with other people. On the organic level, it is the state where the absence of awareness of the body gives way to the feeling of perfect physical well-being. "It's feeling one's body to know that it's all right."

This well-being is experienced or conceived as an abundance, sometimes a superabundance, of energy and of bodily potential reaching its maximum; this applies to capacity for effort and indefatiguability. "It is to feel oneself strong and to be able to make any effort, to be able to take part in sport, be able to keep awake, to feel always on top, not tired, not to be aware of any weakness."

Similarly, conceiving speed of reaction: "It is the capacity to react quickly, to step oneself up at times, to go three times as fast, to run ten times as fast, to act."

Contrary to what the term would seem to imply, equilibrium carries the possibility of excess and abuse. (This characteristic of health has also been pointed out by various authors, especially by Canguilhem, 1950, and Stoetzel, 1960.) To be in equilibrium is to be able to employ the body to the point of abusing it; it is, in the last resort, to be able to allow oneself anything. It corresponds in fact to a disequilibrium between the demands and the constraints of the environment, experienced as minimal, and the reactive capacities of the organism, experienced as unlimited. The normal state is therefore that in which one can go beyond the norm, and we might apply to our subjects' conceptions the saying of Canguilhem: "It is the possible abuse of health which lies behind the value which is accorded to health." (1950, p. 82.)

This casts light upon the relation and continuity between equilibrium and the reserve of health; the former is the actualization of the latter. Equilibrium is characterized by the fact that it goes beyond the purely organic level of the reserve of health and bears upon all aspects of the individual's life, especially the psychosocial aspects. It indicates both the state of the individual and his mode of life; the organic state acted, experienced and used by the individual in his relations with his environment.

These relations are characterized by their harmony and by the individual's control of them. Thus, if equilibrium is often regarded as a synonym of activity, what is involved is a kind of activity at once unstrained and effective. "I think equilibrium supposes a continuous state of activity . . . it is optimism, to want to do something, a kind of continuous dynamism." "When in the morning you wake up fresh and in good shape, when you have your mind on your job, when everything looks rosy, when work is no bother."

Evenness of temper or good humour are thus always implied, sometimes in association with the mastery of difficult situations, sometimes with good relations with others. "People with good health are often very happy, they may be gay, they can be good company for others."

Finally, in the last resort, equilibrium becomes linked with individual freedom. "It is to be able to act so as to do what you want to do, to live how you want to live, i.e. to be completely free."

If the idea of abundant physical capacity seems at first glance to be incompatible with illness, equilibrium, in so far as it is not merely an organic state but also a kind of behaviour and a mode of relation to the environment, may nevertheless encompass certain limited disorders. We can understand in this sense the person who said: "For me, there is no such thing as perfect health, it's much more a matter of being able to keep a balanced life . . . to be slightly ill, for example to have a tendency to bronchitis isn't to be in bad health, nor even having mild attacks of asthma. I'm in good health when I am in equilibrium, when I feel myself capable of doing what I want."

Equilibrium accommodates these disorders just as it accommodates excesses. It is not compromised by them because it is on another level. As long as the individual keeps the same relations with his environment, he is in equilibrium despite physical disorders. As an "optimal" state, equilibrium is not confused with the "perfect" state.

We hope that we have succeeded in casting some light on the two main characteristics of equilibrium: firstly, its normative character; and secondly, the field it covers, including the individual's whole life from purely physical to psychosocial aspects. After the "being" of health-in-a-vacuum and the "having" of the reserve of health, equilibrium rather represents "doing". Its two aspects are linked: if equilibrium is a superior form of health, representing the norm, this is because it goes beyond the purely physical, because it is a norm of life as well as a norm of the body.

This analysis of equilibrium is similar in some ways to the interpretation of health given by some writers as a normative, ideal thing, a kind of limiting case rather than an actual and statistically common state. In particular, Canguilhem writes:

> As if perfect health were not a normative concept, an ideal type. Strictly speaking, a norm does not exist, it plays the role of depreciating the existing to enable it to be put right. To say that perfect health does not exist is simply to say that the concept of health does not refer to something which exists, but to a norm whose function and value is that it be compared with the actual so that the latter may be changed.
>
> 1950, p. 39

For Canguilhem, as we have already said, the real meaning of health is to be found in the possibility of excess, in going beyond customary norms or in establishing new ones. Health is also for him a state which is not confined to the physical but includes the active mastery of the environment: "We must look beyond the body to appreciate what is normal even for the body itself." (1943, p. 124.)

Canguilhem, however, seeks to define perfect, absolute health, an ideal concept which he contrasts with actual states—relatively good, average or poor health—descriptive, according to him, of the state of the individual. Equilibrium, on the other hand, as conceived and expressed by the subjects of our investigation, is not absolute health. It is a form of health, complementary to the other two, not to be confused with perfect health. Equilibrium may include illnesses. The notion of perfect health had apparently no psychological meaning for our subjects. Although rare, equilibrium corresponds to a kind of experience in the individual; the idea has therefore some descriptive value. But it serves to indicate an aspiration rather than a reality, an absence rather than a presence. The experience to which it refers is an exceptional one, and is thereby felt more intensely and valued more. Its value and its normative function would appear to be a consequence of its rarity and of the intense way in which it is experienced, as mastery of and harmony of relations with the environment.

It would thus seem that, despite the apparent unambiguity of the term, we are a long way from having an unequivocal notion clearly defined by its opposition to illness; the various forms of health have different characteristics and functions and entail a variety of relations among them, and between them and illness. The situation is summarized in the Table below.

	Health-in-a-vacuum	Reserve of health	Equilibrium
	Being	Having	Doing
Content	Absence of positive content	Robustness and strength Resistance to attacks	Physical well-being Good humour Activity Good relations with others
Relation to person	Impersonal fact All or nothing	Personal characteristic Measurable, variable and permanent Secondary awareness	Personal norm All or nothing Immediate awareness
Relation to other forms	——	Basis of equilibrium	Based on reserve of health
Relation to illness	Destroyed by illness	Resistance to illness	Assimilation of disorders

Some order, however, can be found to underlie these various dimensions—from absence to presence, from non-personal to personal, from fact to norm. A double frame of reference may be discerned. On the one hand, there is the organic. Here, health appears as a state of the body, a relative state, defined in terms of illness, by the absence of illness or resistance to it. On the other hand, there is the behavioural or psychosocial. Here, health is defined as a mode of relation of the individual to his environment. It is in the interaction of these two aspects, and in the transition from one to the other, that we find that progression which leads from absence of illness to true health, to equilibrium.

5

Illnesses – Dimensions and Limits

Illnesses and their classifications

The problem of classification of illness has sometimes occupied the attention of ethnologists. Frake (1961), analysing the diagnostic of disease in a Philippine people, shows the existence of an exhaustive classificatory system, composed of mutually exclusive categories divided into sub-categories of increasing degrees of specificity. Thus, the category of wounds is distinguished from that of skin diseases in which inflammations and ulcers are distinguished, and where the various kinds of inflammations and of ulcers are further distinguished, and so on.

Also, the distinctions and groupings made in our interviews are strikingly unsystematic and partial, and marked by the heterogeneity of the criteria used. These tentative classifications, however, seem to show an appreciable degree of regularity; they correspond to an organization of the phenomenon of illness in which an attempt is made to resolve the contradiction between the too abstract unity of the entity illness and the diversity of specific diseases.

The analysis of these tentative classifications poses a different problem from that of the forms of health, which appeared clearly as specific realities. The types of illness which are compared and the categories which are distinguished are both more ambiguous and more numerous. The undifferentiated concept of health divides into three distinct notions; that of illness seems rather to be diluted.

The classifications appear at several levels. There are attempts to distinguish diseases from other states, such as accidents, physical disability, operation or happenings of everyday life. The nature of the disorder is in this case the question. Also, each state is qualified and different kinds of state are distinguished in terms of various indices involving numerous dimensions: the severity of the affliction, its painful or painless nature, and several indices referring to temporal criteria.

The distinctions made are in terms of discontinuous dichotomous classifications. Each quality (curability, pain, seriousness, etc.) is only vaguely related to the others. Thus, the classification of some diseases (for example, tuberculosis and poliomyelitis) as long-lasting does not necessarily imply anything about them with respect to pain and curability. The discontinuity of these categories can be seen in the actual reasoning of some people; distinctions are juxtaposed without any connecting link. "I can remember mild illnesses and also quite serious illnesses, and illness has also two other aspects—painful illness and painless illness."

Again, the use of closely related terms (chronicity and after-effects, for example), and of categories, one of which includes the other (fatal illnesses within incurable diseases), reflects a conception not of clearly differentiated states but of a rather confused reality. While references to health struck us by the restricted range of the terms used, centred wholly round the term "equilibrium" indefinitely repeated, we have perhaps in respect of illness a superabundance. It is by accumulating such qualifications, categories and indices that an attempt can be made to delimit the various forms of illness.

This plurality of partial indices thus allows the nature of the affliction to be recognized; the distinction between illness and accident, when it is developed, is based not upon some specific quality but upon one or more of the indices used to distinguish between illnesses—the shock and the suddenness of accident. One subject stated: "I think accident is different from illness in the sense that it is much more violent." When asked his views about the presence of after-effects and the irreversibility of the affliction, the same man said: "I think the experience of accident and the experience of illness are very different; accident often leaves more traces, you take longer to get active again and to recover the use of your limbs, and often you don't wholly recover."

Seriousness may also be seen as distinguishing the two states, sometimes in a holistic way. A clerk, unaware of the paradoxical nature of what he was saying, remarked: "If an accident and an illness are equally serious, the accident is less serious."

The use made of this notion of seriousness is especially noteworthy. This kind of distinction is most commonly expressed by doctors and patients, and recurs almost inevitably in their dialogue. It shows the same uncertainty. As in the case of accident, the systematic examination of its use shows that we cannot regard the term "seriousness" as having an unequivocal meaning, or even as having an independent meaning of its own; it always reflects something of the other notions used to distinguish between illnesses.

Most frequently, seriousness is associated with the danger of dying. "A serious illness, that's cancer, an illness you die from, that's the only thing that's really serious."

Sometimes, seriousness is associated with the duration or length of the illness. "A serious illness is something which lasts for some days or months, or which comes back."

The seriousness of a disorder is also identified with its irreversibility, and with the idea of after-effects or of a permanent change of the organism or of the subject's behaviour, even if it is a minor change. "There are obviously serious illnesses which may have long-term consequences, which involve a falling-off in physical resources, which leave traces, while others may be benign."

The seriousness of an illness is not therefore something specific but indicates an accentuation of one of the features of a disorder, varying with the disease in question—incurability in the case of cancer, for example, but duration in the case of tuberculosis, which is considered most frequently as curable. Seriousness thus appears as the frame of reference in which different indices assume order and take sense for each specific disease. Moreover, when we consider the illnesses which are being classified rather than the classificatory system itself, we see stable associations emerge between a disease and one or several designations. Diseases are located in terms of the intersection of different indices, together with a certain organic content.

Influenza and *tuberculosis*, to which certain common symptoms are attributed, are contrasted on the temporal dimension and on the dimension of serious or benign nature. *Tuberculosis* and *cancer*, on the other hand, are both serious illnesses and are distinguished in terms of being curable or incurable. This in itself is quite banal. It does, however, enable us better to understand the nature of the organizing process involved. Each disease is given an attribute which serves to actualize it and give it meaning and shape. Seriousness thus plays the role of a super attribute expressing the relation of the individual to the illness rather than simply the nature of the illness itself.

This is the real meaning of these distinctions and the principle behind this pseudo-classification of illnesses is to arrange their characteristics not in any absolute sense but in terms of the ways in which the individual is involved in them. If, in fact, we examine the nature of the attributes used and recognized as significant, we shall notice how greatly they differ from medical or, more generally, organic classifications. They are not related to the etiology of the illness, except perhaps in the distinction between illness and accident, whereas most medical classifications are based upon this criterion. Furthermore, they include no reference to anatomical-physiological localization; no distinction is made, for example, between diseases of the digestive system and diseases of the circulatory system. There is no reference to the body, to the organic. Similarly, we have seen that distinctions in terms of pain are relatively rare; and there is no reference to anything objective or impersonal.

The attributes used, on the contrary, have all the function of indicating the implications of the illness for the present or future life of the individual, and the way in which the person is involved in the illness. These attributes must be regarded as indices of personal involvement rather than as objective indices of organic attack. This quality is especially apparent in the various distinctions made in terms of temporal aspects. Let us see what some of the people we interviewed said.

"The important thing is the duration of an illness, an illness of several days doesn't pose any special problems, a long illness can completely transform your life." In this case, the issue is the effect on the life of the individual patient. In other cases, the issue is rather the relation of the patient to his illness. "You can have a temperature which goes on for several days, then you know there's certainly an illness incubating. It's the symptom of something wrong inside, an infection . . . while if you have a sudden illness which leaves you helpless, as when you are knocked down by a car, well, that's something you don't expect."

In the case of accident, also, the suddenness of the attack is significant because it implies, in fact, that the individual is not responsible. "In the first place, accident is something you can't foresee while I think there aren't many illness which don't begin slowly. As a rule, an illness gives a little bit of warning and you can try to stop it at the outset, while with an accident, you can't do anything, you can't really do anything, other people have to act for you."

If we regard these distinctions as representing indices of personal involvement, their multidimensionality, partial character, discontinuity and confusion are of little significance because their function is not to simplify the multiplicity of diseases, but rather to render it meaningful by defining the relation to the individual in each case. The variety of individual relations and responses to illness is implicitly present in these classifications of illness.

To conclude this analysis of "healths" and "illnesses", we may perhaps attempt to distinguish certain general trends.

1. We first noted a fragmentation of the entities health and illness, implying that the relations between these two cannot be reduced to simple symmetrical bipolarity. Our attention has constantly been absorbed by the multiplicity of states and the nature of the notions which reflect this diversity. The forms of health are organized according to three concepts and three distinguishable modes; the plurality of illnesses is organized but not simplified by the attempts which subjects make to qualify these states, to differentiate among them and to classify them.

2. Secondly, we have seen that descriptions and classifications are made in terms of a double frame of reference. The characteristics of the states themselves are regarded in terms of their intrinsic and organic character. Also a "personal" or psychosocial frame of reference can be used. Here, states are characterized and distinguished according to their effects on the person and his life. Equilibrium is a mode of life as much as a state of the body, and it is the relation of the individual to various illnesses or afflictions which provides the basis for distinguishing among them.

Illness in health: the intermediate state of fatigue

In addition to states of health and illness, other states are recognized which may be referred to as "intermediate" (this is the term used by Leriche, 1936, among others). These may be analysed firstly in terms of their relation to health and illness, and secondly in terms of the concrete content attributed to them. The experience of fatigue is dominant, either alone or in association with indisposition or depression. The predominant notion is of a multiplicity of diffuse and persistent disorders. "There are the little troubles, the little situations of discomfort which you have more or less all the year round, headaches, the after-effects of alcohol, digestive difficulties, fatigue . . ."

There are interminable comments on the various states of malaise and depression, especially on fatigue. "Fatigue is mainly not wanting to get up in the morning, getting out of bed saying: What's the matter with me? I feel as if I hadn't slept last night. Feeling as if you were dragging yourself along, not really wanting to do anything, being anxious."

Although the picture may often appear confused, there seem to be three aspects involved.

1. Naturally, the limitation of activity, of physical and intellectual possibilities, is the first, but it appears most frequently associated with depressive phenomena. "I get states of nervousness and irritability which are often connected with this physical fatigue and lassitude . . . depressions, because you feel you can no longer do what you were doing, or when you don't get on as well as you ought to have, or you are too slow."

2. Attention is also given to describing the difficulties and discomfort which this fatigue creates in relations with other people. One person's fatigue is a problem for others. "It isn't nice for a husband to find a snivelling wife, always tired, in an armchair, refusing to do anything outside the usual routine, and that kind of thing can sometimes cause dissension in a family."

3. On the level of experience, some people describe a quasi-permanent state of fatigue. "I'm tired from the time I get up in the morning; when I get to work an hour after getting up, I could just go to bed, I'm in no shape to work, I'm lifeless, without energy, the battery is flat, so to say . . ."

Others contrast their daily experience of fatigue with their lack of experience of illness. "I'm very seldom ill, I regard myself as pretty strong, I'm very seldom out of action . . . but I know very well what it is to be tired, unfortunately."

Others, again, insist upon the frequency of fatigue in the population as a whole. "Fatigue is the state in which more or less everybody lives."

There are theories—especially that of Durkheim—in which the distinction between normal and pathological is based upon statistical criteria: what is frequent is regarded as normal and provides a criterion of health, what is infrequent is regarded as abnormal and provides a criterion of illness. In fact, our analysis of health has shown that norm and frequency of occurrence can be separated. Equilibrium, the norm, is rare. Similarly, the intermediate state, which is frequently found, is not regarded as normal. Indeed, it would appear to be its very frequency which gives it this non-normal quality; it is most often those who mention the commonness and permanence of fatigue who emphasize its abnormal nature.

Only two people, in fact, stated unreservedly that it was normal to be tired. "I need very little sleep. For several months I've slept only six hours a night. From time to time, obviously, I feel a bit tired, it's normal, it wouldn't be right if one were never tired."

This evaluation of fatigue as normal or abnormal draws a distinction between a physical, muscular form of fatigue and a nervous, intellectual or moral form. It is the latter form which people claim to experience, and which is regarded as abnormal. "The fatigue after two or three hours' walk in the woods, you come back and you're tired, but it is a fatigue which doesn't overwhelm you, it doesn't have any serious repercussions . . . while nervous fatigue, I think you feel this rather like an illness . . . men who have too many irons in the fire, they feel fatigue, you see them even in the morning, white and drawn, nervous, with stomach cramps . . . that's a kind of fatigue which isn't normal."

Need we insist upon the fact that this is blamed upon urban life?

Perhaps more important for our purpose than the analysis of the intermediate state itself are the relations between the intermediate state and health and illness. All subjects agree in asserting that the intermediate state is neither one nor the other. In this state, one is neither quite ill nor quite well. "There are any number of people, you can't call them ill, you can't say they're well either. They'll always have something not quite right, the constant fatigue of migraines which don't go away or of little things which mean that they're not as active as they ought to be."

A closer analysis reveals two aspects. On the one hand, the intermediate state precedes illness in time, giving forewarning of it. "There is a condition of liability to illness, of fatigue when you feel illness is going to come, when you prepare for it and get ready for it."

The intermediate state and fatigue thus indicate an increased vulnerability to illness (we are not here considering the questions dealt with in chapter 1). The intermediate state is then a stage in the conflict which is going to result in the starting up of the disease. But there is a second aspect of the intermediate state when this is regarded in a topological rather than a chronological sense, as located between health and disease. From this point of view, the intermediate state is an ambiguous state, reflecting a conflict in the person between health and illness, but a permanent conflict which may go on indefinitely without ending either in the re-establishment of equilibrium or in the outbreak of an illness. "Good health for me is something I don't know much about, in the sense that I always feel tired, with a whole lot of discomforts, things which prevent you expressing . . . it's a kind of spider's web around me, I have the feeling that I've never been ill, but I've never been in really good fettle . . . the term 'old crock' just fits me down to the ground."

What is undermined by the intermediate state is thus equilibrium, true health and full realization. The intermediate state is contrasted simultaneously with illness and equilibrium. On the other hand, not being *an* illness, it does not exclude health-in-a-vacuum. In this case, what does the permanent experience of fatigue mean, if not that there is hardly such a thing as real health in the sense of genuine equilibrium, and that for most of us there is only the negative state of health-in-a-vacuum, free, it is true, of disease, but not of these little ills which make up the intermediate state? This state represents the inexorable challenge to health within health itself.

To analyse the relations of the intermediate state to health and illness is, in fact, to try to define the nature and bounds of these phenomena; after one has studied the different types of health, illness and fatigue, the problem arises of the criteria and boundaries defining the states themselves. We find that some people have the idea of a frontier zone which corresponds precisely to the intermediate state. "There is certainly a frontier zone . . . at a given moment in time, the state of health must be getting less and the state of illness about to appear; at this moment, one is rather between the two, rather in the frontier zone . . ." It is difficult to fix limits for this zone. Although for this person there may be a certain continuity between the states, the boundary is no less difficult to establish.

The idea of continuity may also occur in the form of a difference of degree between the intermediate state and illness. "You can have a mild intestinal infection, the beginning of a stomach ulcer, mild irritation after eating some food, discomfort, certain pre-symptoms . . . if you are in poor physical condition and your resistance is low, these little things develop into an illness." For this man, the intermediate states consist of the appearance of the phenomena experienced in illness, but at a lower level; they have not yet reached their full development. Magnified, but otherwise unchanged, they will constitute the disease itself; pre-symptoms will become symptoms without any change in their nature. In the ideas expressed by some subjects, it was possible to detect an echo of the positivist theories of Comte and Claude Bernard on the continuity between normal and pathological phenomena, the pathological being distinguished from the normal only by a difference of degree, a "hyper" or "hypo" activity. Again, the very notion of intermediate state suggests the idea of continuity; its fluctuating nature and the difficulty of defining boundaries precisely support this view. But, because we have continuity, can we conclude that we also have homogeneity? (It was Canguilhem who drew attention to the distinction between continuity and homogeneity in relation to normal and pathological phenomena and demonstrated that one cannot legitimately apply to the one conclusions drawn in respect of the other.) We can do no more than speculate a little on this point, but when we think of the state as the individual experiences it and not of isolated phenomena, we have a predominating impression of qualitative change and of a kind of break. The symptom may simply have increased in intensity, but the subject's state has changed: he is ill. "I'm inclined to say that the important point in an illness is the moment when you admit to yourself that you have to go to bed . . . up till then, you didn't feel very well, you weren't quite up to things, but you led a normal life. From the moment you take to your bed, you're ill."

In spite of the diversity of diseases, in spite of the fluidity of the intermediate state, there is nevertheless a threshold in actual experience. We thus find ourselves faced with fundamental questions. What is illness? What is health?

6

The Sick and the Healthy

Whatever the range of types of health, of illness and of intermediate state he distinguishes, the individual nevertheless interprets his own condition as one of "health" or of "illness". What are the crucial characteristics which form the basis of this interpretation? How is it that people go beyond the diversity within each state and endow these states with the specific meaning of health or illness?

The need for interpretation appears in relation to illness. Health, as we have seen while examining the processes involved in its genesis (see chapters 1 and 3), is a "given", a matter of fact; indeed, sometimes it is an unnecessary concept in that one is unaware of one's health (see chapter 4). Illness, on the other hand, in so far as it is not a "given" but is acquired and developed in the course of conflict, is for the individual a problem which requires some kind of answer. Illness is something for interpretation and analysis.

Here some relevant questions may be posed: Am I ill? What is illness? Where does it begin? The individual answers by enumerating signs and listing the characteristics of the illness, and wonders about their crucial significance.

This questioning concerns various aspects which, in their heterogeneity, define the content of the experience of being ill. It covers physical symptoms (such as temperature and the external manifestations of the illness), and more subjective aspects such as pain or fatigue. Other aspects are more concerned with the consequences of the illness for the person, his psychological integrity and his behaviour—changes of mood and disposition, being reduced to inactivity, having to be looked after.

Again, however, we find two axes of reference, one strictly physical, the other having to do with the person, his psychological make-up and his behaviour. Three-quarters of our subjects view illness simultaneously as a physical reality and as a kind of behaviour: it is very rare for anyone to give illness only a purely physical content. Moreover, a detailed analysis shows that it is not to the purely physical that the individual looks for his criterion. It is, on the contrary, the shifting of the physical onto another level, that of the experience of the person and his behaviour, which forms the vital reality of illness.

Death

We may well be surprised at the scarcity of references to death as the ultimate reality of illness. Only a few people think that illness is truly defined by the potential presence of death, and begins with this danger. "Rheumatism isn't a disease because a disease makes you die, with rheumatism, you live to be a hundred, it's a warrant for a long life, so it isn't a disease."

Equally rare are those who professedly associate the idea of illness with that of death, and who say, for example: "When I hear the word 'illness', the word 'death' comes into my mind almost immediately."

The majority refuse to envisage the presence, even latent, of death in illness. This denial takes various forms; the fatal nature of a disease is certainly recognized as a criterion of classification (see chapter 5, and in particular the analysis of "serious" illness), and the fatal diseases are distinguished from the others. But by this very act, the fatal diseases are distinguished from diseases in general and the idea of death is dissociated from the idea of illness. People say: "Fatal illnesses are still a minority among the others."

The danger of death, however, is not recognized as a criterion, for the illness starts, people think, well before the danger of death. "You can't associate illness closely with death; most of the time, you're ill without being in danger."

People likewise say that they don't think of death, don't fear it, or don't fear it any more than the physical misfortune of ageing or infirmity. "I've never been afraid of death . . . I think misfortune is worse than death, because with death, it's only a second and it's over."

The assertion of the inescapable nature of death may finally appear as a last form of negation: being inevitable, death ceases to be a problem and loses—or so one would like to believe—its terrifying character. One old woman expresses it in the following rather incongruous but undeniable fashion. "To pass away is inevitable; suffering is perhaps not so, but as for death, up to now, I don't know anyone who has lived beyond a normal life . . . I'm not afraid of death, I find it quite normal because that's the way it is."

It has, indeed, sometimes been said that "illness, even benign illness, comprises an idea of death, a possibility of death", and that in the unconscious illness is equivalent to death (Valabrega 1962, chapter 8, p. 86). The variety and persistent recurrence of negation are no doubt but the unconscious expression of defence against the anxiety which the thought of death provokes. The relative absence of concern with death in our subjects' views recalls Freud's (1964) notion, according to which one only speaks of death by denying it.

Physical realities and behavioural aspects

Dans l'obscurité qui fait loi dès que la peau est franchie.

(Jules Supervielle, *Le Corps*)

Pain, temperature and "external" symptoms occur quite frequently and represent the physical reality of illness. They all indicate to the individual the presence in his body of health or illness. Now, this physical reality is ambiguous and far from clear; each aspect, every sign is or may be important, but is rarely of crucial significance. Between the illness and the physical symptom, we find only occasionally a relation of equivalence or of implication. On the contrary, the symptom is most frequently conceived as *contingent*. This idea finds concrete expression principally in two ways.

1. In an illness, the symptom may be absent or may remain benign for so long that it is not noticed; the illness incubates without apparent manifestations. This appears frequently in the case of pain. "If suffering were really a warning-bell—'ah! something is happening, I'll have to do something' . . . but often there are no symptoms, that's so for many people who have tuberculosis or cancer."

2. Conversely, the presence of a symptom—a temperature, for example —does not necessarily imply illness, it may belong to another state. Here is one observation: "For children, a temperature, that isn't always significant because children get a temperature of 104 for nothing . . . a little tired, growing, it's not necessarily an illness."

The physical symptom, however, when it is present, most frequently plays the role of alarm signal. It draws attention to a dysfunction. But subjects frequently emphasize its indeterminate or partial nature. The individual suspects that he is ill but does not know with what illness. Thus pain only indicates the possible localization of a disorder the nature and origin of which most frequently remain uncertain. "Often by chance, you discover that a headache indicates something wrong with your teeth, or that a pain in the stomach indicates something wrong with your kidneys; it isn't necessarily localized."

Some diseases, of course, are an exception. Mothers of families say that they can recognize the symptoms of childish illnesses. Similarly, the symptoms of a cold or influenza appear unequivocal. And finally, a man may have learned to know the symptoms of "his" disease. "I have arthritis . . . obviously, I see that something's wrong when I am suffering more . . . I know these symptoms." But is it merely a matter of chance that the same man continues: "But I don't really call that a disease because it's chronic; for me, it's something I know, which is a part of my life."

It appears that the notion of illness prevalent in the representation, the picture people have of "real illness", is accompanied by a feeling about the ambiguity of the physical aspect as experienced; people may not be aware of their disorder, and even if they are, they may not be able to read the signs confidently. Subjective awareness of a physical ailment does not constitute knowledge. This is the basis of all the mistrust with regard to the informational value of symptoms.

Illness does not reduce to its physical aspect. For the individual, it is a situation which implies behaviour of two kinds: special attention and recourse to the doctor on the one hand, and being rendered inactive on the other. Illness appears to some as the situation in which it is necessary to "look after yourself". "When you go to see the doctor, and you have to take care of yourself, take medicine, go on a diet . . . cases like that are really being ill."

More frequently, however, we find references to being *reduced to inactivity*. By this is meant essentially interruption of the professional or family activities of the individual, much more than the motor aspect, like immobilization in the strict sense of the word, or being confined to bed. In a way parallel to the analysis of physical signs, we may analyse the nature of the relation between inactivity and illness. Now illness most frequently *implies* inactivity. "Illness is when it prevents you from doing anything, the children for example, measles or scarlet fever must be counted illnesses because they have to be so many days off school, this means being off work, whether for an adult or for a child, well then, that's an illness."

Being off work is an institutionalized stopping of activity. Inactivity is defined in terms of one's role in society. If inactivity is caused by illness, then illness becomes defined in terms of inactivity; to be reduced to inactivity is for most people the real criterion of illness.

The relation between them may be a quasi-linguistic one of strict equivalence. Illness and giving up one's activities are interchangeable and synonymous in communication. "I've never been ill, I've never been off work."

Idleness also sometimes has the function of acting as a *signal*, and people assert its validity. The organism will confirm it later. "Sometimes, I feel I'm not going to continue in good health, simply from a wholly internal impression—wanting to do nothing . . . When this feeling of wanting to do nothing continues, I feel absolutely certain then that there's something not quite right, and this feeling always turns out to be justified."

But most frequently, it has a kind of general significance. Unlike the physical signal, it does not reflect any particular disorder, but indicates illness as a whole; it marks the passage from one state to another, the *threshold* of illness. Its significance is firstly chronological. "I'd be inclined to say that the crucial moment in an illness is the moment at which you recognize that you've got to go to bed, the moment at which, in short, you recognize that you are ill. Up to that point, you didn't feel very well, you weren't up to things, but you led a normal life. From the moment you take to bed, you are ill."

Being off work is also the threshold of illness in another sense; it enables one to distinguish between illness and the intermediate state, or to differentiate between "true illness" and ailments with not much more than nuisance value. "You don't get through life without minor ailments; my husband had an abscess in the throat, but you know, he was never ill, never off work."

INACTIVITY AND RECOURSE TO THE DOCTOR

Illness most frequently reveals itself, not by a single symptom, but by several symptoms which then have to be related; now, the information provided by several symptoms seems no less ambiguous and no more definite than that provided by a single symptom. One of our subjects, a technician, describes it thus: "There are illnesses which make you aware of them by pain, and others by fatigue, and also by high temperature. Basically, there are three indications—temperature, which is easily found out; pain, which is similar; while in the case of fatigue, you don't really know whether there's anything abnormal going on. For example, take tuberculosis; this is a disease which doesn't seem to be doing any harm and often you realize that you're ill because of a bit of a temperature. Obviously, there are cases where one can be tired simply because of not getting enough sleep or from overwork. A pain might come from an old scar which becomes painful when the weather changes . . . so pain is an indication, but not one you can depend on, in fact, like fatigue; in this case, you can try to verify by means of temperature, although there are also illnesses in which you don't have a temperature . . ."

We find the subject progressively more uncertain when faced with phenomena which seem to him more and more ambiguous. In this case, no single phenomenon has an unambiguous significance; it is not possible to define the illness unambiguously from one symptom alone. But the information provided by several symptoms does not improve matters. The individual assembles them together without reaching a clear pattern. The illness persists in eluding him.

It has often been emphasized that anxiety in the face of an illness arises mainly from uncertainty, from "not knowing". Brissaud (1892) in *Histoire des Expressions Populaires Rélatives à l'Anatomie et à la Médicine*, states: "The need to understand is so compelling that it may actually out-do the desire to be cured." Balint (1957, chapter 3, p. 25), likewise, insists on the desire of patients to give a name to their illness. It is within this perspective that we must view the significance for our subjects of having recourse to their doctors and obtaining an indication of the diagnosis of their illnesses.

The physical, indeterminate and unclear as it is, becomes the doctor's concern. It is for him to organize this confused complexity and give it meaning. He must "define" the illness. There are numerous accounts of how the patient rids himself simultaneously of his uncertainty, his anxiety and his body when he goes to the doctor. Our data do not add anything new here, but confirm these interpretations of the patient–doctor relationship. "You feel there's something not working right and you think, Hullo, I've got something. You don't know exactly what. Some people say: 'It'll pass.' For myself, I'd rather go straight and see a doctor because I want to know."

The idea of a preventive medical examination, which appears sometimes, is likewise associated with the ambiguity of symptoms. "Myself, I rather think the Americans are right, that's to say . . . every two years they make a thorough examination of your blood, with every kind of analysis, and at the same time a general 'check-up', that is teeth, eyes, the senses, nerves and so on. This enables them to check their general condition, even if they haven't any symptoms . . . you shouldn't wait for symptoms, because when there's pain, the disease is already well advanced."

It must be added that all uncertainty is not abolished by the doctor's diagnosis, for we also find: "I went to see a doctor, he examined me, and found urea . . . but I'm a bit sceptical, these troubles I've mentioned, they're still there, I feel them from time to time and I never felt the presence of urea in my blood at all. Do they even know what the symptoms of urea are? . . . Well anyway, they told me I had urea . . . I had to be satisfied with that."

The doctor plays the part here of "constituter" of the disease, giving meaning to the symptoms and deciding between what is part of the illness and what is not. This is not the only way in which the function of what we may call coordination is performed; behaviour may play the same role. Paradoxically, it is inactivity which gives meaning to physical symptoms and which makes a significant pattern out of a diffuse complexity. "I had a bit of a temperature, I was exhausted all the time, I was losing weight, but I didn't pay much attention to it, I went on with my life and one fine day, they said to me, 'You'll have to give up work', and then I said to myself: It's serious, you're ill."

In fact, as long as one's activity is unhampered, physical phenomena are perceived but not thought of as illness, while the sense of being ill arises when everyday activity becomes difficult. "The attack of malaria I'm talking about, I hesitate to call it illness . . . it wasn't an illness for me, because I took advantage of it to do a whole lot of things I didn't have time to do otherwise; the time I really found distressing was the three weeks following, when I forced myself to carry on my normal life without being capable of it, without being capable of normal activity. That was really when I felt I was ill."

INACTIVITY, PAIN AND PSYCHOLOGICAL STATES

Physical signs acquire meaning according to the limitation of activity which they involve. Such limitation also gives rise to the psychological changes taking place in the patient as a person. A comparison with pain may be relevant here. On the level of subjective experience, inactivity is regarded as the most important aspect of illness; it is said to be even more important than pain. One subject comments as follows on his experience: "I suffered a lot with a stomach ulcer, but that didn't affect me very much, whereas the rheumatism which kept me in bed for three months and again the following year had a tremendous effect because it's not so much the pain which matters as the fact of being immobilized."

Changes of mood and personality sometimes appear in association with the experience of pain. "Continued suffering has surely an important effect upon the personality, people who suffer from stomach trouble or acidity . . . when they always have the same discomfort, day after day, their personality is affected by it."

Pain is thus the only physical aspect with the character of a global phenomenon, affecting the psychological make-up of the person. Most frequently, however, changes of mood and personality are associated with, and arise out of, being reduced to inactivity. "I've very often been ill, I've been confined to bed for several months, I was cut off from the outside world, I was very downcast and pessimistic, everything I heard made me feel dismal."

This subject, a bachelor, is thinking only of the physical isolation of the patient in bed in his room. A young mother of a family sees inactivity as giving up her maternal role. Thus inactivity may also lead to isolation in a sense very different from the purely physical. It breaks one's ties with other people. "If I were seriously ill, if nothing more could be done, then it would be finished, family life wouldn't exist any more . . . I couldn't look after the children any more, and at that point I'd be cut off from my family; life would have to go on without me."

A new but essential dimension appears here: relations with other people and the changes in these relations which are consequent upon illness. These are associated with inactivity. The experience of illness thus goes beyond the physical level and affects the individual's whole life, his relations with others and his social status. Such changes occur

D

because of inactivity. Thus inactivity would seem to be the idea—and the experience—mediating between the physical and the psychosocial aspects of illness.

The behavioural content of health, as we have seen, is as obvious as that of illness. Equilibrium is a way of life rather than a state of the individual. If inactivity is the true criterion of illness, then, conversely, true health consists in behaviour and in active control of the individual's environment and of his relations with other people.

While the discontinuity and ambiguity of symptoms reflects in some measure the diversity and fluctuating nature of organic states, illness and health, on the other hand, appear clearly defined in terms of a behavioural criterion. The real criteria of illness and health involve the whole conception of the person, his behaviour and his relations with other people. They are behavioural and have a general significance rather than being physical and specifically localized.

Physical facts, symptoms and dysfunctions have, of course, an existence of their own, but they only combine to form an illness in so far as they transform the patient's life. While each sign conveys information about some particular disturbance and emphasizes the diversity of different conditions, the interpretation of signs and their integration into the notion of illness takes place in, and through, behaviour. Health and illness are delimited and conceptualized on this level.

The unity of *meaning* provided by behaviour—the unity of illness is in contrast with the ambiguity and diversity of *signs*—the diversity of illnesses. Activity and inactivity thus enable us to define health and illness in terms of conduct and no longer as states. They are essentially the kinds of conduct characteristic of the sick person and the healthy person, with unity and meaning.

REPRESENTATION AND MEDICAL CONCEPTIONS

If we compare, even in a very summary way, the conception emerging in the social representation with medical conceptions of illness and its symptoms, we may first note certain points of agreement. For both doctors and laymen, illness has many aspects and does not reveal itself by a single critical sign but by a multiplicity of symptoms which have to be organized into a whole. The doctor shares his patient's mistrust of subjective perceptions of physical signs. Canguilhem writes:

Morbid symptoms as subjectively experienced and objective symptoms rarely coincide. All is not mere fancy for the urologist for whom a man who complains of his kidneys is a man who has nothing wrong with his kidneys. [. . .] The well-known fact of referred pain . . . prevents us from thinking that the pains patients bring forward as major subjective symptoms have any direct connection with the viscera to which they seem to draw attention, but above all, the prolonged latency of some degenerative processes and the non-obvious nature of some infestations or infections lead the doctor to regard the patient's direct experience of pathological processes as insignificant . . .

1950, p. 48

We find, in fact, all the arguments used by lay informants in questioning the value of physical symptoms. For both doctor and patient, a translation process is necessary to determine the objective reality of what is indicated by the subjective sensation. This is the function of medical examinations. From a different point of view, Balint (1957) shows an identical mistrust. The doctor must often "refuse" the physical symptoms "offered" by the patient, and will only be able to understand the nature of the trouble if he takes account of other phenomena, i.e. the patient's vital psychological problems.

Again, for both modern medicine and popular thinking, illness is a molar phenomenon and a vital phenomenon, and, in consequence, goes beyond the isolated physical fact. For Canguilhem, health and illness are norms of life; illness is "another way of life" which can only be clearly recognized on the level of the oneness of the individual. Similarly, Leriche (1936) defines health as "life with one's organs silent", and illness as "what makes it difficult for men to carry on their normal everyday life".

The recurrence of identical themes is striking. But these do not have the same meaning in the social representation and in medical conceptions. For the doctors, the multiplicity and ambiguity of symptoms and the many forms illness may take constitute the phenomenon itself. This must be understood and action taken accordingly, whereas in the thinking of our informants, the lack of clarity regarding the physical aspect seems to result in a kind of unreality. One subject, for example, said: "Signs and discomfort and all that, I don't believe much in that because it's so difficult to interpret them."

That "signs" may appear as matters of belief is in this respect significant. Again, in regarding illness as a molar and vital phenomenon, the doctor seeks to give a richer and wider meaning to physical facts, while we may, as we shall later see, interpret the individual's recourse to behavioural criteria as an attempt to deny the physical reality.

SOCIAL REPRESENTATION AND SOCIOLOGICAL DATA

We again find the same themes in the results of some sociological investigations, whether these are concerned with the way in which patients interpret their illnesses (for example, Pratt, 1956; Pratt *et al.*, 1958; Suchman, 1964), or with the perception of physical symptoms and the behaviour which these initiate in the subjects (for example, Hoffer and Schuler, 1948; Koos, 1960). Both kinds of investigation recognize that one cannot treat a symptom as in itself a satisfactory criterion of illness. Each symptom is perceived differently by the individual according to his system of values and his relation to his social group. Both kinds of study agree in questioning the excessively "realist" conception of illness. "The idea of illness arises," says Stoetzel, "because some people say that they are ill, and say that they are ill because they are authorized and even encouraged to do so by those about them." (1960, p. 614.) We may therefore distinguish, as do Mechanic (1960) and Mechanic and Volkart (1961), between the illness itself as an object fact, and "illness behaviour".

The conceptions we have referred to tend in the same direction; the difficulty our subjects experience in finding a criterion in the purely physical indicates, as we have said, a degree of unreality in illness. The fact that inactivity—interpreted in the sense of not going to work, of giving up one's social role—integrates the physical symptoms, indicates that it is in relation to one's social group that symptoms acquire meaning.

The comparison of our own data with the results of these different studies enables us to clear up an important point. Illness behaviour, however it may be defined, is regarded by these authors as the result of, and the proof of, the fact that the symptom is perceived and identified as illness. Our own analysis suggests that we should reverse the terms. It is because it leads to behaviour that the symptom becomes a sign of illness. Whatever the effective dynamics of the process, as far as the social representation is concerned, the consequence actually comes first. The individual evaluates his condition not according to its intrinsic manifestations, but according to its effects.

Different factors, such as the pragmatic perspective of some researches, the social importance of the doctor, the theoretical and practical importance of doctor–patient relations, have contributed to the fact that studies have been essentially concerned with the seeking of medical attention. Going to the doctor is regarded as the prototype of illness behaviour (Mechanic and Volkart, 1961). In our data, going for medical diagnosis and therapy sometimes seems to be what defines the *condition* of illness. According to Valabrega: "Illness is something which occurs between the patient and the person who is taking care of him." (1962, p. 25.) This definition seems in accordance with the social representation. However, it is not the dominant idea. It is the notion of inactivity which defines most frequently and, perhaps, most "primitively" the fact of illness. Illness is first and foremost the condition which obliges the patient to interrupt his normal activity.

We shall return to the question of illness conceived as inactivity or as seeking attention (see chapter 8). Here, we shall examine what the two definitions have in common rather than contrasting them. In both cases, illness is defined by the relation of the patient to a third party— to the doctor or to the function of the illness. Medical diagnosis and interruption of activity both represent the intervention of society. By these means the individual becomes "a patient" *for the other*, that is, for the doctor, for his professional colleagues or his family, and *for society*.

The sick and the healthy

Health and illness are defined as behavioural universes, as forms of conduct and no longer as states. When, however, we question people about the validity of behaviour as a criterion, these forms of behaviour are no less ambiguous than physical facts. In particular, all illnesses do not immobilize the patient to the same extent; some involve only minimal restrictions, or none at all, on activity. Different people with the same physical condition behave differently; some interrupt their activities, others do not. Some look after themselves, others do not. But these facts, which our informants recognize, do not lessen the crucial importance of behaviour. On the contrary, the very idea of illness is defined as a function of such. Illness begins when in a given physical condition an individual behaves as if he were ill, and, conversely, the individual who, in the same physical condition, does not behave in such a way, remains healthy.

Behaviour, especially inactivity, as the criterion and threshold of illness, is an individual criterion and threshold. It is not important that it varies with each individual because its value as a criterion remains unaffected. If the variety of conditions finds a kind of unity in the behaviour of the patient and the healthy person, such behaviour must not be conceived as universally defined, but as essentially fluid, according to the needs, possibilities and situations of different individuals. "Illness is everything which makes the individual incapable of carrying on his life normally . . . somebody with a cold generally carries on . . . but if he's a fraud, he won't be able to work, and then he's ill."

This view of a kind of individual health and illness comes near to that of some scientific conceptions. For Canguilhem (1950, Part 2, chapter 3), too, "being ill" can be defined only as an individual norm for a given individual. But some views go further: they propose that the norm is the act of the individual himself. A norm is a norm *for* the individual but also a norm *of* the individual who decides, in a debate in which behaviour is both outcome and arbiter, whether he is ill or well. This is clear in all cases where we can see a conflict between physical condition and conduct; in continuing to act like a healthy person, in spite of his troubles, the individual retains the status of a healthy person. "Some people, when they have 'flu', act as if they didn't have it. You say to yourself, 'It's a bit unpleasant, a germ', but you don't make it into an illness, that's what."

The individual's defence (cf. the analysis of individual characteristics and their role in the genesis of illness discussed in chapter 1) here assumes the form of denial. Some subjects, talking about their illnesses, expressed the opinion that illness was something that could be overcome. They said that they behaved exactly as if nothing was wrong and thus felt this to be the case. Many subjects seemed to think that if you had sufficient will-power, illness would not make you into a sick person.

From this point of view, we can better understand certain difficulties in the patient–doctor relationship. In particular, light is cast upon the cases of hypochondriacs, in whom their subjective symptoms do not reflect any objective disorder. To the doctor who tells them that they have "nothing wrong with them" they oppose the evidence of the change in their mood and behaviour. They know they are ill by these criteria and the negative results of physical examinations are therefore meaningless. The norm of the patient is opposed to that of the doctor; for the individual it is no less clear and certain. Conversely, the doctor might qualify as "healthy in their imagination" those people who, strong in their continuing activity, reject the meaning and name of illness as applied to their physical disorders.

We must now emphasize the implications of being reduced to inactivity. The patient sees the disintegration of the assembly of different tasks and responsibilities which were his and which constituted his role and defined his position in his social group and in society. It is in relation to other people and to society that activity and inactivity acquire their meaning, and the healthy and active are differentiated from the ill and inactive. Beyond the diversity of individual experience and conduct, a social group of "sick persons" is constituted by the fact that they are accorded the same position in society; a group of individuals excluded from the everyday world, or rather, living in a different world. However this may be interpreted, whether with favour or with distress, people believe in a world of illness, differentiated from the world of health.

The world of health is a social world, the world of the active individual integrated into his social group. In the world of illness, the individual is no longer defined by what he does, but by the inactivity of the sick person. The usual laws of society no longer operate; the individual is relieved of the demands imposed upon him by society, but also risks being excluded from it. This is the situation which the sick person has to confront.

The analysis of our subjects' conceptions has thus led us from notions of illness and health as different physical conditions, to notions of the sick person and the healthy person, defined in terms of their conduct and their respective positions in society. Through the introduction of the relation to society, we find the conception of a social group of sick people, and of a world of illness and a world of health. We may judge how far we have come from the diversity and ambiguity of individual physical states to the unity and symmetrical polarity of the sick and their world on the one hand, and the healthy and their world on the other.

Part 3

7

The Social Representation of Health and Illness

Genesis, conditions and conduct

Whether we are concerned with the genesis of health and illness or with their forms and criteria, we have a guiding schema in that health and illness are always thought of in association with two other notions: those of the individual and society.

The social representation is built up on the basis of these four terms. Thus the conflict between the individual and society finds expression in the states of health and illness. Conversely, these states are defined as health or illness only as referring to an individual in society. The resulting system of relations may be represented as in the Figure below.

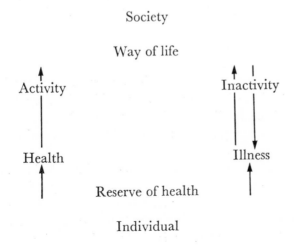

We may now look at the process of genesis as follows. Illness arises from the conflict between society as mediated by the way of life, and the resistance of the individual which we have called the "reserve of health". The result of this conflict will be either illness or a victory for health. The relations between the two pairs of terms are therefore in a sense parallel. Society is opposed to the individual as illness is opposed to health.

$$(\text{Society}/\text{individual}) = (\text{Illness}/\text{health})$$

But it is in the assimilation of society and illness, on the one hand, the former finding expression in the latter, and of the individual and health on the other, that the social representation of the genesis of health and illness takes shape.

$$(\text{Society} = \text{illness}) / (\text{Individual} = \text{health})$$

Similarly, the subjective experience of health represents integration in society through activity; the experience of illness brings exclusion via inactivity. Indeed, the states of health and illness, which are in themselves obscure, acquire meaning through the social behaviour of sick and healthy persons.

This schema brings together, in dynamic interrelation, the essential notions which our subjects used to take account of reality. It shows us how the image of reality is structured and how the notions of health and illness then emerge. In the course of this "operation" on reality, the two-fold contrast of health–illness and individual–society, in short, has the function of providing the stable conceptual framework of the representation.

On the basis of this attempt at synthesis, and of our whole analysis, several observations may be made.

Health and illness appear in various guises. Illness can be regarded as a "state" of the individual, as an "object" external to him and finally as the "conduct" of the sick person. Health can also be thought of as a state, something belonging to the individual, and as the conduct of the healthy person.

Health and illness are more accurately distinguished and defined not as states—for these are often confused and poorly delimited—but in terms of their genesis. Illness as an external "object" is contrasted with health as a property of the individual; and in terms of conduct, the conduct of the healthy person is contrasted with the conduct of the sick person.

The relation between the two pairs of ideas is different in these two cases. In the case of genesis, we have clear and well-marked contrasts. Health and illness appear as quite different concepts, and the individual and society confront one another in an apparently irreconcilable conflict. And further, these two pairs of contrasting terms are relevant to one another, for the conflict between health and illness reproduces that between the individual and society from which it is derived.

As far as conduct is concerned, on the other hand, the subjects' conceptions indicate an adjustment of the individual to society. Behind the most clearly defined notions of the conflict and struggle between these different aspects of reality, we find indications of exchange and adjustment. The relation of the individual to society ceases to be one of adjustment to an external reality. If he can be said to be excluded from society by illness, he forms part of it in so far as his health is good. Views of health and illness are no longer restricted to expressing the relation between the individual and society; they become functionally related in the form of the conduct of the sick person and the healthy person.

Similarly, health and illness lose their character as clearly defined aspects of reality. Illness, by ceasing to be the object of society, ceases to be something outside the individual, and becomes the behaviour of the sick person. On the other hand, health, as an expression of the individual, binds him to society. The world of health is the social world. Health and illness likewise cease to be entirely different things, and become two poles of individual experience. Health and illness are at opposite ends of the dimension, but are defined in terms of the same criterion of activity.

There is, nevertheless, a certain asymmetry between health and illness. The genesis of illness is two-fold—the individual acts in response to the pressure of the way of life. Health, on the other hand, is entirely an individual thing, produced and used by the individual, and never something outside him.

On a different level, the social conduct of the healthy person is the direct consequence of his individual condition. The link between the individual and society is a single one in the case of health; it is a double one in the case of illness (see Figure on p. 91). The behaviour of the sick person is the result of the illness created by society, and also represents a response which may deny the illness and oppose society (cf. the attitudes of denial of the organic state by carrying on activity described in chapter 6).

This all suggests that illness represents a more complex phenomenon than health, in its genesis, and in the behaviour of the subject. Health, which is the simpler phenomenon, is the expression and extension of the individual. And, through health, the individual fashions and moulds the society around him by his control of the environment.

To this asymmetry in the social representation there corresponds a difference in the awareness and conversation of the subjects. Illness is a source of problems and therefore the object of awareness and communication. Health is, as such, the absence of problems and thus of awareness and communication. The excessive amount of talk about illness contrasts with the relative poverty of reference to health.

The study of the behaviour of the sick person and the healthy person cannot be separated from the conceptions of health and illness which we have seen emerging. We shall now see how the conception of a social object orients attitudes and behaviour with respect to that object. The behaviour which defines the sick person and the healthy person varies, as we have seen, in terms of activity and inactivity; but it can also be analysed at two other levels.

1. It may be viewed as behaviour oriented towards health and illness, that is hygiene behaviour with respect to health and the special attention necessitated by illness.

2. We may also view the conception of the sick person and of the healthy person as models of behaviour and personality for the individual. Health and illness influence the individual's perception of himself and of others and shape his entire behaviour and relations with his social group. An essential aspect of this is that health facilitates adjustment to the way of life and participation in society. In contrast, illness liberates the individual from the constraint of the way of life and from participation in society. We must interpret the behaviour of the sick person and the healthy person with this in mind and we can best understand why their behaviour should be different if we take this into account. This difference in fact will reflect the diversity of forms and of meaning which the individual's relation to society can assume for him.

We shall first examine hygiene as behaviour with respect to health and illness—for health and against illness—and we shall try to show how the variety of "hygiene behaviours" acquires meaning when it is viewed as mediating between the individual and his way of life.

We shall then examine three models of illness behaviour corresponding to three conceptions of the sick person and the healthy person in society.

Hygiene

The behaviour of the healthy person may be identified with the activity of the individual in society. Behaviour for the preservation of health finds expression in the practice of hygiene, which represents an attempt to deal with the harmful way of life. Rather than make this effort, however, people often aspire to a life in which health would be in no way threatened and would not require any special kind of behaviour, in which harmony would come about naturally between man and his environment. This is thought of as the ideal way of life for health.

Life in the country is most frequently referred to. We have already considered (see chapter 2) its quality of complete antithesis to the urban way of life. For the few country dwellers questioned, however, life in the country is not an aspiration but a reality. And they judge it in a rather special way. The majority of them appreciate, as do the town dwellers, the rhythm of their life and the good air, but their overall attitude may be different. We have already mentioned the case of a young boarding-house owner who regretted leaving the city and in fact believed the complete quiet to have an adverse effect on her state of health (see chapter 2). Conversely, a postmaster, of Parisian origin, who had been living for several years in the country, fully shared the views of the city dwellers. "My state of health is much better here in the country . . . in Paris, I led a rather nervous life . . . here, you have to take it easy, you get a different rhythm . . . the air is very bracing here, by the seaside, and then I eat at regular hours, which wasn't possible in Paris . . . I do a bit of gardening and I eat the vegetables from my garden."

The case of the city dwellers is different. We may wonder how far this return to nature corresponds to a genuine deep-seated aspiration, and how far it may be only a matter of words. All we have to guide us is what we can glean from a few particular cases. There seem no grounds for questioning the sincerity of a taxi-driver, obsessed by the fear of cancer, who remarked: "Myself, I feel that I'm in a pre-cancer state, a state favouring the development of cancer, and if I had the chance of getting away from Paris and the surrounding area, I feel I'd recover something of my vitality, in particular, a kind of equilibrium which would let me put up an effective struggle and not get cancer after all."

In some people, however, the Utopian nature of such aspirations is quite present, and their attitude one of imagination and make-believe. For example, we have this journalist: "If suddenly I had, let's say 800 F. F. a month assured income, without any questions, . . . I don't ask for the moon . . . enough to let me shut myself up when I felt like it, in my little place, and produce two books a year . . . I think I'd keep well because I'd be doing a congenial job in healthy conditions in the country."

Among others, again, doubts appear. After describing at length life in the country and all its advantages, we find attitudes typified by the following comment: "Of course, it can't be such fun every day, there are drawbacks, all the same, I believe that the closer you get to nature, the nearer you are to the real thing . . . but could I get used to it?"

Still others seek a "compromise" solution between the two opposites of city life and life in the country. This seems to consist of an attempt at juxtaposition. "The ideal would be to do the kind of work you do in the town, but to be in the country . . . at the seaside, especially, where you have fresh air and a restful life . . . near Saint-Nazaire, it's a big industrial town, there were people living at Pouliguen some miles away, they came to work in the factories at Saint-Nazaire . . . I think that's the ideal."

In spite of—or because of—its quality of being the exact opposite of city life, life in the country constitutes an imaginary solution only. Apart from a few special cases—two people only mentioned a specific project for leaving for the country—it is a case of a Utopia the role of which seems to be to reinforce the negative image of our actual life and to disparage it still further. We also find attempts to explain this desire for a healthy life. "I think the need to get out of Paris, to have a change of air and a healthier life is really more the need for a change in one's life. Everybody has a desperate need for holidays, it's not so much the need for a change of scene as the need not to do what they are doing."

At the same time, life in the country is not the only way of life ideal for health. Other aspirations appear such as managing city life, or a creative life allowing the individual to express himself in his activities and interests. These visions have a similar Utopian quality; they do, however, indicate an attempt at integration and adjustment to city life. However unsatisfactory city life may be for the individual, he cannot escape from it; he therefore hopes to find, in the strict sense, an acceptable *modus vivendi*. Is this not the significance of the value attached to health? To allow the healthy person to adjust to his way of life? These imaginary solutions also indicate that our way of life might itself contain the resources necessary to correct its defects. Technology, the "modern" aspect of urban life might not, in certain conditions, automatically generate unwholesomeness and constraint. After the alienation of man by technology, we here find the reciprocal theme of his liberation by the very same means.

Hygiene is not a Utopia but an actuality; it is not an aspiration but a solution. It does not form a way of life but it is composed of specific, known behaviours which bear on various aspects of existence. These behaviours appear more or less possible and desirable in our urban way of life. They can be followed, rejected or neglected as the case may be.

People reject or ignore some health measures while adopting others; this may be firstly a matter of individual needs. "I've got a good digestion and I don't bother about what I eat, but I can't work if I haven't slept well, if I don't get my regular sleep." Also the requirements of the way of life are involved. These various modes of action may be more or less open to the individual. "When I eat in a healthy and natural way, I know a very great difference in my health, in what I do, but . . . with the kind of life I lead, I'm not able to watch what I eat."

It is paradoxical to find the representation, common to all, of the unhealthy way of life finding actual expression in such a great individual diversity of health measures. By their function in the conflict between the individual and his way of life, however, these acquire rather more general meaning. Before examining them, we shall first try to describe the diversity of the measures themselves.

The most frequently mentioned concern eating. The detailed attention to every aspect indicates that this is probably the area regarded as most important. "Certainly you have to watch what you eat. The system is like a machine, like a car, when you feed it with good petrol, it goes better . . . the cells renew themselves from what you eat . . . I think food is terribly important."

To watch and correct one's diet, not to eat too much but to eat enough, to choose certain foods and avoid others; all these things seem psychologically more "present" for the individual than, for example, the more habitual body hygiene. In this field, people take pains, or think they ought to take pains, and also believe that these are effective.

"I pay attention to how meals are made up, for example, if the vegetable is starchy, the entree is light, grated carrots or olives or something like that. According to the meat, I vary; whether that's done in sauce or grilled, I take care that the vegetable isn't like the *hors d'oeuvre*."

Sleep is equally important. Subjects say, for example: "As long as I sleep my usual eight hours undisturbed, I'm all right." But sleep is not the only kind of rest people find necessary; a number of health practices seem to be founded, more or less explicitly, on the idea of relaxation. Trying to find relaxation is also, in itself, an important theme. "What you need is to get yourself relaxed, for example if all day long you're in high gear, you have to get relaxed again by a degree of comfort in the evening, at home, which enables you to relax in one way."

Some kinds of behaviour—practising a game, going out into the fresh air, going away on holiday—are also seen as ways of achieving relaxation. Indeed, bodily hygiene itself sometimes appears to have this significance. People say: "A bath is a physical and mental relaxation."

The search for relaxation, in all its forms, thus represents the second main field of health behaviour, after eating. Bodily hygiene itself, keeping clean and attempts to prevent illness are much less frequently referred to and come only in third and fourth place.

We may wonder whether in actual practice more importance is attached to healthy eating habits than to cleanliness and medical prevention. After all, there have been, in the interview situation, certain taboos preventing free communication on matters of bodily hygiene. (Perhaps the fact that women spoke more freely of bodily hygiene to female investigators should be regarded as an indication of this taboo. This can also be related to the frequency of reference to children.) But one thing seems certain: concern with eating—when it exists—constitutes a personal preoccupation which is more conscious and more constant than bodily hygiene and medical prevention, which is to a large extent institutionalized. Again, both preoccupations appear frequently in connection with the care of children; they must be taught to keep themselves clean, and prevention is most important for them; on the other hand, it is just as if, for the adult, whatever the effective habits may be, keeping oneself clean is no longer a problem, while eating can remain a personal preoccupation all one's life.

We should not, in any case, be surprised at the importance accorded to healthy eating in a conception in which illness results from the invasion of the organism by entities from without. The food ingested by the organism is one of the essential bases for the unhealthy nature of the way of life; to be careful about what one eats is, according to this theory, to take direct action to control the assimilation of that which is unhealthy, and thus to prevent disease. Conversely, "good food" brings or reinforces health.

The importance accorded to food in relation to health is indeed a very old idea; the notion of "food-health" or of "food-medicine" has for long been attached to certain products, such as wine. In our data, we find the theme of "natural" food being better than remedies in the form of chemical medicines. "I get very tired eyes; the doctor gave me drops, but I preferred to see that I was eating properly . . . nourishing things, healthy cooking . . . these drops, they would have caused irritation rather than anything else."

We shall not go further examining the various forms of health behaviour; it is not our aim to provide a systematic inventory of current practices, but rather to unravel the meaning of hygiene in relation to health, illness and the way of life. We shall therefore attempt to analyse its function in the social representation.

The significance of hygiene derives from its function in the conflict between the individual and his way of life. It represents a possible line of action for the individual, faced with the incursions of the way of life, and it is from this point of view that we shall see emerge the representation of hygiene behaviour for health, beyond the diversity of particular kinds of behaviour. The effects of hygiene are positive.

Hygiene provides an effective response to the way of life, but it plays the part of a palliative. It does not transform an unhealthy life into a healthy one, but it makes it tolerable. It does not allow the sick person to rediscover health, but it prevents his condition from getting worse. It can enable the healthy person to avoid illness, and it increases, especially in children, the capacity for resistance. Such a vision is certainly a positive one. However, hygiene is not accorded a universally applicable function. Only rarely do people regard it as necessary in all situations, and "natural" to the individual. Most frequently, it is seen as relative, specifically called forth by the incursions of the urban way of life, and thus as having a here and now value only. "Hygiene is something which is necessary in the light of the situation in which one finds oneself."

We also find: "Hygiene isn't natural to man, animals don't need hygiene."

Some people say that hygiene is needless in the country. "I lived a completely different life in the country; people there, in short, don't have any bodily hygiene. . . . You weren't ill there, not at all, because there you're in a healthy place, while in the town, a person's body runs far more risk of toxic residues; I think that in the town you have to use hygiene . . . in the country, perhaps not."

To aspire to another way of life is also to aspire to giving up health behaviour which has become pointless. Life in the country is an ahygienic ideal. It is certainly true that country dwellers are more guarded. One we interviewed said: "It's as necessary to have hygiene in the country as in Paris."

This difference is readily understood. Country dwellers do not always have as definite a picture of their life as Parisians; and hygiene corresponds to the harmful aspects of their way of life.

The requirement for hygiene measures also depends upon the individual's state of health; they are important when it is affected or at least threatened. Whether he is ill or tired, the individual will have recourse to health measures. One of our subjects stated: "A really healthy person doesn't have to bother about endless precautions."

Health measures thus form part of the "unhealthy way of life—illness" world, while they are absent from the world of the healthy man with a healthy way of life. Their presence in the representation, however, permits variations in the rigid schema of conflict between the individual and his way of life. Health measures are induced by the way of life but are also a form of response to it. Our picture of the genesis of health and illness becomes more flexible; the individual emerges from his purely passive role. He finds a mode of action. Further, illness loses its quality of fatality; thanks to health measures, it can be avoided.

Health measures thus appear to have a double mediating function: between illness and health, for health and against the threat of illness; and between the individual and the way of life imposed upon him. They nevertheless allow the individual to overcome and adjust to his way of life. Health measures resolve the paradox of having health both threatened and required by our social life.

We may understand the fundamentally ambivalent concept of health behaviour on the basis of its mediatory function, that is its function as a means of compromise between the aspirations towards the healthy life and the need to adapt to the unhealthy conditions of everyday life.

Health measures are a *need*; that is why they develop out of the situation created by the way of life. This "neutralist" conception is particularly relevant to care in the matter of food. In the other cases, the connection between health measures and the person oscillates between two opposite meanings. For some, health behaviours, or some of them, correspond to a *preference*. The individual takes pleasure and finds satisfaction in carrying them out. Naturally, this includes such activities as sports and, in general, everything to do with relaxation, but the taste for health is not restricted to such things as these. It may also include bodily hygiene and even eating habits. "For me, paying attention to what I eat is quite natural, I don't calculate calories or vitamins, but I take care. Really, I take pleasure in it; it's quite likely that if I didn't enjoy it, I might not do it."

To the necessity created by the external situation is added the satisfaction of a need which is the individual's own; health measures constitute a response directed against the way of life, qualitatively of an opposed kind and therefore satisfying. Opposed to the constraint of the way of life we have the free exercise of and pleasure in health behaviours.

The contrast is particularly marked by statements such as the following: "Necessity imposes a certain amount of health behaviour on the individual. . . . Here, it's not preference that's at work but reason; you have to exercise self-discipline and for food, I think you simply have to look after your health." A technician summarizes this notion of *health-discipline* perfectly for us when he says: "Health measures are a discipline for oneself and one's body."

As in the case of "health-preference", every health practice may appear to the individual as an effort of discipline. Paradoxically, however, those connected with rest or relaxation are among those most frequently affected by this sense of discipline. We are concerned here with two opposing conceptions of health behaviour, and with its double relationship to the person and to his way of life, rather than with a typology of health behaviour.

When health measures become part of a body of rules—there are some things which one must do or avoid, and neglect or refusal takes on the meaning of failing to obey the rule—the individual may find there the satisfaction consequent upon obedience or the reassurance that comes from doing something effective, but in either case, he can scarcely be said to take real pleasure in what he does.

In spite of their beneficial effects, health measures are, in effect, one more constraint imposed upon us by the way of life. This leads us to what we shall call the "health paradox": in response to an unhealthy and constraining way of life, the individual must have recourse to practices themselves constraining and unnatural. The response to the way of life is now no longer a "response of opposition", but, on the contrary, is "the same kind of thing" and thereby may lose its character as something genuinely satisfying.

Health practices thus appear as techniques, implying, it is thought, an education. They are a kind of learned behaviour, and as such regarded as opposed to natural, spontaneous behaviour. "That kind of thing depends on the education of the person from childhood. You have to be used from childhood to taking care over bodily hygiene. If somebody is let go at the beginning, he'll be like that all his life."

People also sometimes think that health practices require knowledge and methods. "In modern foods, you have to take account of experiments on foods, and to know their food values and the results they can have. You really have to take account of the scientific knowledge which has accumulated in these fields."

That means measuring and apparatus. "I know people who weigh every ounce they put on their plate. I think that's terrible. And then, they weigh their eggs at table because they mustn't weigh more than so much." In this last statement, made by the mother of a family, we see rejection: beyond certain limits, health measures may come to be regarded negatively. If their unnatural, technical, constraining nature is too much emphasized, they cease to be regarded as a response to the way of life and come to be viewed simply as an expression of it.

This rejection—or at least, reserve—finds expression in the conception of health measures purely as a *social norm* without any real objective content. This is especially the case with respect to bodily hygiene. "For some people, to have a bathroom, they feel absolutely obliged to have a bathroom in the house."

We then find this referred to as a modern health facility, a facility for big towns, and it is judged to be obligatory, excessive. "Bodily hygiene seems to me to get too much attention in the big towns. It's abnormal, it seems to me, to have a bath every day. I think it's not right. Personally, I have a bath every week, I think that's enough."

It is in such cases that, from being beneficial, they become pointless and even harmful. The identification of health measures with the way of life is then complete. Like the way of life, health measures are not only constraining but also threatening. "I think the modern and ultra-modern health measures in Paris are a bad thing."

While moderate health measures reinforce children's "reserve of health", exaggerated health measures weaken it. Over-protected children are sickly. "You don't want too many health measures, you mustn't badger children because they have dirty hands. I think children have to get toughened a bit."

This view is an extreme one, shared only by a minority of our subjects. It does, however, help us to understand the meaning that health measures can have in some cases, and well indicates their ambiguous nature. For the majority, nevertheless, we can discern a kind of spontaneous solution of the dilemma, with the idea of health measures as *personal norms*. Health measures should not be the same for all, but personal, individual and adjusted to the needs of each. This point is in fact insisted upon most emphatically in relation to attention to food. "For each person, his diet, he has to be able to say: 'Is this good for me? Is it bad for me? I'll stop taking it'."

The variety of individual behaviour acquires meaning in this context. Health measures lose their constraining character; from being something imposed, they become something chosen, from something common to all, they acquire an individual character, from being identified with the way of life, they find a fresh identity as personal attributes. They can therefore play their part as mediators between the individual and his way of life. At the same time, the individual's potentiality for action is increased. Knowing his needs and his weak points should facilitate more effective and flexible action if health measures cease to be automatically applied general rules. For the individual, to find the dietary regime or rhythm of sleep which suits him, and the health measures suited to his own nature, is to resolve the conflict between the healthy and the unhealthy, between homogeneous and heterogeneous, and to resolve the original conflict which illness involves.

8
Conceptions of Illness and Illness Behaviour

Health and illness are experienced and thought of by the individual in reference to society. Through health and illness, the individual takes his place in the constraining society, or is excluded from it. This is essentially the view of Parsons (1951) who views health and illness as demand and response in the functioning of the social system. Health is necessary to the system. "A little reflection will show immediately that the problem of health is intimately involved in the functional pre-requisites of the social system. [. . .] Too low a general level of health, too high an incidence of illness, is dysfunctional." (p. 430.)

Conversely, illness is a form of *deviance*, motivated by the demands made by society on the individual. The "sick role", i.e. the norms of behaviour which society, i.e. those in contact with the patient and, in the first place, his doctor, validate, the "institutionalized anticipations" relevant to his behaviour are, according to Parsons, a mechanism which canalizes illness as a form of deviance. Can this interpretation help us in our examination of illness behaviour? Is being ill perceived and experienced by the individual as a deviant position in society, and is health perceived and experienced as conformity? Is the function of the behaviour of the individual patient to canalize deviance, as the Parsonian analysis would have it, or is it, for example, to exploit it?

It is, as we have seen, through the activity of the healthy person and the inactivity of the sick person that the relation of the individual to society finds concrete expression—participation or exclusion, perhaps conformity or deviance. Three modes of organization of the representation can be distinguished according to the meaning the individual attaches to inactivity, or three conceptions of illness—involving models of behaviour in relation to the illness, to treatment measures and to patients—corresponding to conceptions of the relation of the individual to society.[1]

Our analysis does not involve the actual behaviour of the individual but the norms which he reveals and his interpretation of them; we are not concerned with the real relations of social exclusion or participation but with the conceptions of these relations which are expressed. The three kinds of conception of illness are: (1) illness as destructive; (2) illness as a liberator; (3) illness as "an occupation". In terms of these the individual expresses his relation to illness—or to health—as this relation is established in society, and his relation to society as this relation is established through health or illness.

Illness as destructive

Illness may be thought of as destructive. This conception, as an examination of its content will show, seems characteristic of persons who regard themselves as particularly active or engaged in society. For each of them, the essential aspect of illness is inactivity, which has various implications. Giving up one's professional and family role, financial problems, being excluded from one's social group, all nevertheless have a common factor of meaning: the desocialization of the patient. "You feel almost left out of society."

Two main features seem to be involved.

1. The subject who recognizes himself to be ill feels inactivity and believes that the loss of his social role has been imposed upon him, that it is a kind of violence inflicted upon him. One man, immobilized for life by an accident, said: "For me, who am forcibly compelled to do nothing, the most painful thing is to see others working and not to be able to do so too . . . because I've worked all my life since I was young and now . . . it's rather hard to bear, not being able to do anything."

[1] Our approach was firstly to define 'key-themes', i.e. formulations differing in respect of the meaning of the social inactivity of the invalid for the person concerned. These themes express a complex relationship of individual–illness–society or individual–health–society. They thus function as differential criteria for the different conceptions of illness, and form the basis for a classification of interviews. It should be noted that this classification, made by two individuals independently, was by no means perfect. For one thing, some interviews (12 out of 80) turned out to be unclassifiable. For another, a number of "mixed" interviews were found in which more than one view of illness was expressed; except for the purpose of "illness as a liberator", these have been omitted from the analysis. We then analysed the interviews falling into each group. The account of each notion of illness represents a selective description of the data, as well as a theoretical model of an essentially indicative nature.

Another patient, without any stable occupation, tells us of his professional failures: "Unfortunately I've been asthmatic since I was four. Well, that made it difficult for me to study when I was a kid and later too, it prevented me from doing what I wanted to do . . . there are jobs I might be successful at and where eventually I'd be thrown out because of my health."

2. Furthermore, inactivity means the destruction of ties with other people, exclusion and solitude. Thus, the patient referred to above indicates that "without a job" he cannot create the social bonds he would like—he is not a worthwhile partner, he has nothing to offer. "It's difficult to think of getting married or starting a home when you don't have a job . . . this kind of thing has vexed me, you know. There are girls who have perhaps kept clear of me, even unconsciously, because I don't have a job." The mother of a family says: "If I were very seriously ill, if nothing more could be done, then it would be finished, family life wouldn't exist any more . . . I couldn't look after the children any more, and at that point I'd be cut off from my family; life would have to go on without me." People also think in terms of exclusion from social life in general. "While I was ill, I got letters from a friend in Paris who was setting up a social centre for young people, who was very active, and I really had the feeling of being useless and all alone." Financial problems are also viewed from this angle. "For the invalid, there's also a problem of money, there's the stopping of the help he may have to give to his dependents; apart from himself, his own personality, he can be reduced absolutely to nothing because he can't help his dependents."

As against this view, which expresses the desocialization of the invalid, some people show, in a variety of ways, their involvement in social participation and the value they attach to their role and to the efforts it requires of them, something akin to a kind of valuing of health and of the efforts necessary to keep it. "In so far as it's important for me, I try to keep in good form . . . I have an exacting daily life, that is, I have a certain number of things to deal with in my work and I make a point of dealing with them and consequently, I'm careful for that purpose."

Similarly, the individual sees himself in his role, wholly identified with his function; he insists upon his responsibilities. An administrative officer says: "I've noticed that people who have responsibilities, like me, certain people, all my friends, are often less ill than others. For example, take the case of 'flu' in winter, well, generally speaking, the administrative staff have less 'flu' because someone with responsibilities, who cares about his work, gets worried, he feels himself to be irreplaceable, and then he'll say to himself: 'If I give up, I don't know what will happen'."

The feeling of being "indispensable" in one's role is important. "At that time I was working in trade unionism . . . I had an enormous amount of work to do and I said to myself: 'I really don't see who else could do this job, it's got to be done, it's essential so whatever happens, even if I'm ill, I won't give up'."

The persistence of behaviour characteristic of health whatever the objective state of health exemplifies the most important thing about a person's role: to assure the individual of the permanence of his social function and to preserve the essential identity between it and him. The individual is therefore wholly located in a social universe, as a personality identified with his social role, which requires health and rejects illness. Illness here is indeed clearly a form of deviance.

We must now try to understand how personal disintegration results from social deviance. An examination of the individual experience of illness will be highly relevant. Before examining each aspect, we may indicate the general sense which is that the invalid, excluded from communication with others and rejected by society because of the loss of his social role, cannot rediscover a place and a role as an invalid. Nothing in the form of life which is illness allows him to do so; hence illness is wholly negative.

Thus, inactivity is declared intolerable, but, at the same time, the few activities possible for the invalid are devalued, and cannot act as a palliative. A technician tries to envisage what the experience of being ill would be for him: "To be stuck in a bed, not to be able to get up would be terrible. Obviously, you can read, but you can't read all day, to read like that isn't an activity. I have a rather active disposition; there are people who settle down to illness. For myself, I don't know if I would hold out long. I've an idea that for me, it would be very serious morally. I think I'd give in pretty quickly."

Almost always associated with inactivity there appears a theme which is equally important in defining the status of the invalid in our society: his dependence on others. Just as, for these people, inactivity is intolerable, dependence is distressing for them. Help is unwillingly accepted. "Always to wait for somebody to dress you, to do this and that, that's as irritating as suffering. You suffer morally and other people get fed up with you. I've never liked being dependent on anyone . . . it's not normal to have to rely on other people."

Another notion also appears. There may be no help; the invalid is *alone* in the midst of others. "When there's illness, you are and remain alone . . . there's scarcely any possibility of being helped. If you can't put up with this state, if mentally you're really seriously affected and you don't respond any more, I don't think anyone will help you to respond. That's what's basically so awful, I think, that illness makes you really alone."

Reciprocally, again, the healthy person expresses the difficulty of communicating—or living—with an invalid. He sketches a kind of invalid autism. "When you go into a nursing home, you go into a world which is as spotless and shut off as the nursing home itself, or as the white and gleaming walls of the nursing home . . . there's a series of patients with their problems; there are the nurses running from one to another . . . each patient has his problems, his special routine, his reaction to this routine . . . each patient is a little planet, all by himself, a fastened-up world."

Alone in the midst of healthy people, the invalid further refuses to perceive or to create ties with other patients. They annoy him. "Hospital seems to me the most objectionable place . . . I think the community is the worst thing about it . . . because you already sometimes have enough difficulty in putting up with your own suffering without having to put up with your neighbours' suffering too."

As long as inactivity, dependence and social exclusion appear to the person as intolerable and destructive, there is no solution to be found in illness. Inactive and excluded from the society of the healthy, the subject finds himself inactive and alone in his illness. One cannot take one's place in a world of invalids, or rather, the world of invalids is a world of irremediably solitary individuals.

We can therefore easily understand the appearance of feelings of anxiety in various forms, especially associated with dependence on others. Such feelings of anxiety culminate in expressions of annihilation themes. The connection between the position of the invalid in society, defined by his inactivity and his dependence, and his personal annihilation, is clear. Illness, for those for whom it is a form of social deviance, is non-being, it is a terminus, it is death. "Illness, somebody drags on for years and leads a kind of sub-life, a kind of semi-death."

"Illness is the stopping of the life of the invalid, it's the catastrophe of life . . . then, life is nothing." "I've got the impression that a serious illness which makes you incapable of a normal life is a terminus, an end-point, I really think it's a kind of death." "Illness which immobilizes you, it's a sort of slow death, in fact, bodily and spiritual agony."

We thus see in what sense illness can be called "destructive". Destruction, annihilation and death are not the result of illness, a danger in the future, but a part of the immediate reality which it involves. It is while he is alive that the invalid is annihilated and deprived of any future: he is dead although he still remains alive. Death here is not, of course, bodily death, but social and psychological death. Destruction threatens the personality even more than the body.

Descriptions of the invalid bring in other factors. According to the majority of our informants, the patient is "attenuated". "For me, a person who is ill is a person with a club foot . . . I have a feeling of something not finished, imperfect, the impression that the individual is attenuated."

Some people describe the transformation in more qualitative terms, as a loss of social qualities on the one hand and of energy and independence on the other. The invalid becomes unbearable for other people and becomes so in the way of a selfish and whimpering child. One subject said: "During two spells when I had stomach trouble two years ago, my family could hardly put up with me, I was so demanding and selfish. I couldn't bear anyone." Another claimed: "To be ill is to lose one's energy."

In these cases—when "attenuation" is talked of and when the transformation itself is described—what is being referred to is a process of regression of the invalid, the criterion being, apparently, the autonomous and socially active individual adult. The invalid has lost these adult qualities; he is "less than before". He has regressed to the passive and dependent state of a child, but, whereas the child has his place, as such, in society, the invalid seems, in this view, unable to find any place.

The case of a man asthmatic since childhood confirms this interpretation. It shows how, because of his early illness, he remained fixated—in this case there can be no question of regression—at the level of character and social status of a child. In him, the male adult could not develop. "There's the fact that I haven't a very energetic nature . . . I think that's because potentials of energy within me were stifled by the fact that I was too spoilt when I was a kid, as a sick child . . . and then, a kind of softening process which meant that I had a limited kind of life . . . and there are aspects which followed on from that, that I'd call childish or effeminate."

Another patient, who was suffering from a thyroid dysfunction, refers, in her own case, to a genuine feeling of "depersonalization". She is no longer herself because of her illness, feeling herself invaded by a person of less worth because she has lost the qualities of self-control and effectiveness which belong to the healthy person. "You become a different person, you are no longer yourself, it's as if you were drugged . . . you become another, unknown, revolting, whimpering person who can't put up with anything, who loses control, who is good for nothing . . . it's something inhuman, it's no longer me, it's like these mentally ill people whose writing changes, you are psychologically, spiritually and physically deformed . . . you are ill in every sense."

Further, it is probably significant that those few individuals who envisage the possibility of a beneficial transformation of the person see it essentially as an increasing of the invalid's sensitivity. "When you're ill you're unhappy; when you're unhappy, you're more sensitive."

In any event, we have here a quality of a quite different kind from those associated with the healthy, active, energetic, adult and manly.

The account above provides a picture of illness and the invalid as people actually experience it. We must now examine more carefully the qualities involved, from the cognitive point of view. How are the notions of health and illness defined? One point would seem to be essential. The experience of illness is dominated by the invalid's inactivity, and, similarly, the notions of health and illness are defined mainly by reference to behavioural criteria. This conception, which is characteristic of the representation (see chapter 6), is here particularly obvious. Illness is virtually defined in terms of the reduction of the invalid's activity—and its destructive consequences.

It follows that there is a tendency to restrict the (negative) notion of illness and correspondingly enlarge the (positive) notion of health. Some disorders which do not have a marked effect behaviourally are thought of as belonging in the world of health. Thus, of certain benign afflictions, it is said that they are not illnesses. "I think you can't call 'flu' or a cold an illness, you don't stop what you're doing for a sore throat or an attack of 'flu'; it's got to be fairly severe, something really out of the way like an attack of typhoid or pneumonia where you're really laid low. That's really an illness."

If behaviour is so crucial, it is not surprising that physical phenomena as such only have a limited place in such a view of illness. With reference to all the subjects in our inquiry, those who regard illness as destructive less frequently attach importance to temperature, pain and even death —as a physical phenomenon—when they attempt to define illness (see chapter 6). They are, on the other hand, the most ready to accord importance to the external manifestations of illness and of its duration. The significance of this seems to be as follows. The greatest effects of a disorder on the behaviour and life of a subject are often due to its duration. On the other hand, by its external manifestations, the disorder affects those associated with the patient, as well as the patient himself. The individual recognizes illness in the picture which he presents to others.

There is therefore a clear relationship between subjective experience and the cognitive content of the notion of illness. We must now see how we can fit into this picture the norms concerning the behaviour of invalids.

The relation which develops between the individual and illness may be formulated in terms of power. What can one do in the face of illness? One can, of course, look after oneself and try to overcome the illness. But in the case of "destructive illness" that is not the essential thing. We are struck by the apparent ambivalence between the possibility of denying the illness, and thus seeming omnipotent in regard to it, and total impotence. This contrast conceals another—between physical condition and behaviour. It often seems to be believed that the physical condition can be denied by maintaining the behaviour characteristic of good health. "I carry on exactly as if there was nothing the matter with me."

If health exists as a model of behaviour and personality, physical impairment loses its meaning and its quality of illness. But cure by this means is also possible; in this case, there is omnipotence over the physical impairment, and a complete victory of the behaviour of health over the state of illness. "There are many cases of people who are ultimately cured purely by will-power . . . people who were regarded as being as good as dead and who got better simply because they were determined that their illness wasn't so very serious."

Under the heading of "illness as an occupation" (cf. below, "illness as an occupation") we shall find a very similar idea of the struggle of the patient by his will. People also believe in the possibility of a victory over the physical by such means, but this is achieved through illness behaviour; it is by behaving like an invalid that one is cured. In the present context, on the contrary, the thing is not to behave like an invalid. Whether it is a consequence or a cause, being reduced to patient behaviour indicates powerlessness with respect to the illness itself. When physical condition and behaviour come together, the patient is deprived of all recourse whatever The last step is taken. "Well, if you're in bed with something which makes you only half alive, you can do nothing, you just put up with it, that's what's so awful."

Destructive illness is characterized by the fact that social deviance, personal annihilation and powerlessness over one's physical condition are all involved together.

In this context, behaviour itself can be ordered on a scale (this term is not used in its technical sense) ranging from complete rejection of illness behaviour to complete passivity.

The significance of such rejection is clear. Thereby the problem of illness is resolved at all three levels: that of physical condition, of the person and of social participation. To reject illness behaviour is at one and the same time to get better and to maintain one's life and personality intact through social integration. The maintenance of activity as long as possible is clearly the essential point. "I'd have to be really ill before I'd admit it to myself . . I'd really have not to be able to stand up any more before I'd give in and change my way of life and give up my work."

The refusal to take special care or to go to the doctor also corresponds to a desire to deny illness completely, and the same is true of the refusal to "know" and to find out about one's condition. One subject says: "For myself, this history of tuberculosis, if I'd never known about it I'd have been just as well and I'd have gone on living . . . there's nothing like telling people they're ill to make them even iller. When you know, that's it, you've got 'your' illness and I think that makes it worse, more than anything . . . well, I'm not denying the role of the doctor, you need them, but in their penchant for giving their diagnosis to the patient, I think they go too far."

Denial may be less complete; thus, the rejection of rituals and external signs and the refusal to "establish oneself" in one's illness is less relevant to the actual behaviour than to its manner. The adoption of illness behaviour has to remain hidden or discreet. "When my husband is ill, he doesn't like people to see him taking medicines. He fixes it, he sort of hides, and I actually think it's very important . . . for that not to become an event in the house . . . that creates a kind of state of being ill; you are ill . . . you mustn't establish yourself in an illness." The same person also says: "One hopes it will be a temporary thing which will pass very quickly and normal life be resumed very soon."

This desire is not quite the same thing as the trite wish for an illness to be short. To want to shorten the duration of the illness, to deny it its natural run of time, represents one stage in the scale of denial of illness. Elsewhere, subjects admit, for various reasons, that a certain amount of time will be taken up by the illness. Here, it is only a "dead period", a kind of "suspension of time" that people want to shorten. Special care and going to the doctor when one gets round to it are to this end. So also, people try to deny illness by the magical hope of an almost immediate cure. "I'm very ready to have an operation when it's necessary. I want it done as quickly as possible and I want it to be a radical operation so as to be finished with the business, with this illness . . . I'd like a philosopher's stone which would cure me immediately."

But if the illness becomes established and goes on, the last step is taken. The patient is overcome by "real" illness, which leaves him powerless in relation to the physical and effectively brings about his exclusion and annihilation. Passivity then takes precedence over denial. Psychologically, if not always chronologically, it is the result of a failure of denial.

Denial and passivity therefore appear as the two possible responses to destructive illness. The one is a solution of the problem, representing victory over illness; the other indicates the failure of the person who then makes no further attempt of his own to find a solution but at best waits for a solution to come from outside. The patient gives up. Recovery becomes the concern of others, of the doctor or those around him. He wishes for it but he no longer contributes to it. "I had this attack which kept me in bed for five months; I had everything done for me, without asking me, they made me have treatment, I was shut up in my room, it was annihilation, I simply counted for nothing . . . I got better without knowing how."

Passivity, however, may have another meaning: to be entirely passive is another way of not taking part in the illness. "When you're ill, you have things done for you, you are looked after; but when I'm ill, I don't bother about it myself, I let others bother about it."

The patient rejects annihilation by transforming himself into an

E

object. He rejects the "personage" who has the illness by the final assertion: "It isn't me that's ill."

Illness as a liberator

"A really serious illness is like a first love affair."
(Mlle R, 33 years)

For some people, illness appears as a kind of liberation. As in the case of destructive illness, the beginning is in inactivity. But this time the subject feels it as a lessening of the burdens which weigh upon him. This is the significance which one man gives to rest: "When I'm very tired, I often wish I were ill . . . illness is a kind of rest, when you can be free of your everyday burdens." About abandoning responsibilities he says: "For me, illness is breaking off from social life, from life outside and social obligations, it's being set free."

Sometimes our subjects insisted that there was not only a break away from social constraints but also a blotting out of the everyday, i.e. of reality itself. Illness is the out of the ordinary world. Subjects emphasized its pleasantness. "I felt as if I were discovering another world, because there was a kind of pleasantness about my life which was quite exceptional . . . I had a kind of world apart for myself, something which, in fact, I needed."

Although it is sometimes more threatening, the image is always positive. "Suddenly, everything takes on an entrancing quality not at all like everyday life . . . I think things are new, or become new, undoubtedly because of the presence or threat or possibility of death."

The out of the ordinary may even assume something of the fantastic. "Illness is both painful and marvellous . . . I've got a kind of need of the marvellous, to be outside of a kind of reality I find more or less second-rate . . . it's one way of entering a world which is quite unreal and also almost one of the most important things in life . . . it's perhaps the fact that I want to escape from reality which is such a strong motive, or that I despise it or dread it . . . I think it is . . . the ability to reach this world where you don't really know what things are really like."

There is the same uncertainty in the appreciation of time during illness. Sometimes it is felt as a stoppage of everyday life, when illness is thought of as giving one time. "It's a sort of holiday almost better than the usual kind of holiday."

Some people reported experiencing time in an exceptional and much more meaningful way than in ordinary life. "Everything becomes terribly fast, exciting and interesting when you're ill . . . I feel the days are at the same time both much longer and much shorter. Time has a different tempo and passes differently."

There might be said to be two conceptions of illness as a liberator. 1. In the first, illness, in a more matter of fact way appears as rest, the interruption of the everyday rhythm and of social obligations. It is exceptional only in the objective sense of being rare. This conception corresponds to clearly delimited illnesses—benign, short and painless illnesses which, not being in any way threatening, represent a beneficial pause in the subject's existence.
2. The second and more dramatic conception sees illness as an exceptional phenomenon by its very nature, charged, as we have seen, with more intense significance. It includes serious illness, death and pain.

As with destructive illness, subjective experience and the meaning assigned to it are associated with selective perception and with differential apprehension of actual phenomena. In all cases, however, there is desocialization of the patient brought about by the exceptional experience which illness represents. Illness as liberator and destructive illness therefore have the same starting point. But desocialization in the case of the former represents a very different thing—exclusion from society is regarded not as destructive, but as a liberation and an enrichment of the person. The patient, far from being annihilated, rediscovers possibilities of life and freedom. "You get the feeling of being more alive . . . you have an exceptional and very pleasant freedom, it's a kind of renewal."

Three aspects are stressed.
1. The possibility of intellectual activities permitted by the removal of social obligations. "I certainly had a life of intensive cerebral activity which I should never have had but for this illness."
2. A beneficial effect is attributed to solitude. "When I was young, years ago, tuberculosis was a much more serious illness than it is now. We used to be sent to the mountains for a couple of years, I found that extraordinary because it was a kind of contemplation, solitude . . . I think you can gain from the relief that solitude brings."
3. Reference is made to the power, i.e. the privileges which the solitude of the invalid brings. "It doesn't matter though you're stuck in bed, you have many more possibilities than when you have to earn your

living." This power, however, is also power over others. "When you're ill, you can have much more effect on some things than in your usual life, you can act upon yourself and upon others." One of the fundamental privileges of the invalid is to be accepted by others; to be precise, society accepts desocialization. "You're irresponsible when you're ill, you're entitled to be what you are and you are somebody who has to be protected and respected as such." Some people actually find this tolerance surprising. "The invalid is jolly privileged, incomprehensibly so . . . well, this kind of religion of pity there is toward invalids, even among the most brutal and unfeeling people . . . one mustn't take the death or illness of anybody lightly, society forbids you to."

A more intense life, freedom, power over others and privileges are thus concomitants of the abolition of the social world in favour of the exceptional and superior world of illness. Some subjects asserted their indifference to or their disregard of health as synonymous with the constraints and limitations of life in society. "I've no desire to preserve my health; well, for me it signifies the ideal of the well-adjusted animal . . . I've no sympathy for that animal, it's something contemptible, rather."

Exacted by society, health represents for the individual the requirement to participate in society. "Health is the law, the vital minimum; the health administered by society is a make-shift . . . health is what is required of you every day; that's why one isn't particularly anxious to get better, because health is such a dull thing that if from time to time, there weren't the holidays provided by illness, or just holidays . . ."

The person does not find in life in society the satisfaction of his needs and his aspirations. He asserts himself as distinct from his social role. Similarly, life in society is not the "true life" which is only revealed in illness. Illness, a form of social deviance, is thus "inverted" into an achievement of the person, an inversion not without analogies with that which we find in the representation of the "world without illness". (See chapter 2. Among those people who described illness as a liberator, the "world without illness" was also regarded as impossible and, most particularly, as undesirable.) Health is identified with social constraints and illness becomes for the individual a defence against the demands of society.

On this basis we can see the perception of the personality of the invalid taking shape in three directions.

1. Illness is viewed as a "liberation" of the personality associated with

the lifting of social constraints. "I'm a great believer in the effect of illness on people. It allows them to be what they were before and what they can't be because of social circumstances." Illness is therefore revealing, the individual rediscovers himself, becomes himself, sometimes thanks to solitude, by which the invalid reaches the truth in himself. "During my illness, I was more isolated. That allowed me to recover myself, because I was relieved of all responsibility, no longer having to confront others, I have the feeling that I was much more free to be just myself."

2. But the personality is also transformed in a positive way, and "enrichment" is referred to. In contrast to the conception of destructive illness, it is here the invalid who represents the personality ideal, an ideal which is reflexive rather than active. The experience of illness has a formative value, connected with pain and the threat of death. It encourages reflection, lucidity and awareness, awareness of oneself, reflection on life and its problems. The following is an example of the ideas of a healthy person wishing for the lucidity of the invalid about his own life: "I say to myself: 'If I were very seriously ill, I would see better what to do. If I were very near death, I could take decisions'." But enrichment also takes the form of a greater receptivity to others. "It might be said that ultimately he (the invalid) was better than before, morally, it had helped him, it made him much less superficial, more sensitive, he had a much deeper insight into people." The experience of pain, subjects think, also brings with it a superior form of communication with others. A young woman thus describes her relations with a young invalid: "She suffered, she was a martyr . . . but you know, there was a whole kind of friendship based on that, an impression of something achieved, of an exchange."

3. This conception culminates in the idea that, through illness, there develops an "exceptional personality" which corresponds naturally to the exceptional experience of the invalid. "The invalid grows in stature because he suffers and because he has an experience which others do not have. You can see people who have gained greatly psychologically, who have become exceptional people, who have an experience. I envy them."

If it is easy to describe the personality of invalids: it is nevertheless very difficult to form a clear picture of their behaviour. Indeed, their behaviour matters little to our informants—examination, special attention or relations with the doctor are not the essential thing. At least, we quite often find these regarded from the point of view of ritual. Special attention makes the presence of illness clear to all; the aspects of this attention constitute the rule of life in this privileged world. "When you're ill, you have to drink something or other and it's absolutely necessary and urgent to do so. The only thing you have to bother about is your temperature and that has a special importance which isn't questioned. Things are clearly defined, the things you have to do and the things you mustn't do."

At the same time, it is essential to enjoy illness and to get as much enriched by it as possible. From this point of view, we find a kind of welcome to illness emerging, in the absence of any specific behaviour; it is accepted, sometimes even wished for. "I've always looked forward with pleasure to the possibility of being out of circulation for a certain length of time and to having illness put me in a special world apart."

It is believed that the origin of illness is favoured by the individual himself, in so far as it corresponds to a desire or need. "If nobody wanted to be ill any more, there would be much less illness . . . I believe very strongly in the possibility of starting off illnesses oneself and mis-leading the doctor."

In this sense, there is indeed evasion in illness, motivated by the liberating nature of illness; subjects then insist on the active role of the individual and on his responsibility. His role is not limited to using illness against the demands of society: he facilitates its development. It is just as if the individual could turn back against society the threat which it holds over him.

This conception is found as a unique—and extreme—image of illness only in a few people. For the others, there are several coexisting images. In particular, the image of illness as a liberator sometimes exists together with that of destructive illness. Alongside a predominant assertion of the value of social integration and almost hidden by belief in life through society, the other notion, involving the idea of a benign kind of illness which cannot threaten, makes its appearance. According to this notion, society may also be something which prevents us from living, and the short pause afforded by illness may enable us to envisage another life.

The attitude of others seems here to be crucial. If illness, and therefore desocialization, is accepted by one's associates, a positive conception of illness may be developed. But, when the attitude of others is no longer favourable, and illness is no longer tolerated by one's associates but regarded as a heavy burden, its beneficial nature becomes blurred.

"When your everyday life affects others, when the mother of a family has to say, 'But what will my children do if I am ill?', she can no longer bear to be ill; illness itself here is poisoned by everyday life. It's no longer a genuine illness, it's a problem which prevents other people from being happy."

Society, and the ties and obligations which it creates are thus denied and devalued to a lesser extent than might appear. The invalid can only enjoy his solitude and his desocialization as permitted, or favoured, by his associates. Society has to supervise the invalid's "evasion" for illness to become a liberator.

Illness as an occupation

"Illness is an occupation.' (Mme C, 54 years of age)

Illness may, finally, be seen as an "occupation". This term must not of course be taken literally, but conveys the sense of the conception—the recognized function of the patient is to struggle against his illness. This function has some of the qualities of an occupation. It is prepared for and learned. "From the moment you know what's in front of you, it seems to me the only thing to do is to gather your strength and fight."

Let us emphasize the active nature of this struggle. Illness requires of the patient behaviour which keeps him physically and psychologically active. Subjects insisted on the energy that must be put into it. "You really fight; I fought like a lion; you've no idea how much energy it takes."

Illness is seen not only as the situation in which one is reduced to inactivity, but also as the situation in which one has recourse to the doctor, and in which one takes special care of oneself. From the beginning, there is thus emphasis on the invalid's active fight. Additionally, if inactivity is inconvenient on the professional or family level, it also has a positive function: it is through being freed from the burdens of everyday life that the individual finds the energy necessary for his struggle against illness. (Inactivity here has a very different function from that attributed to it in "illness as a liberator".) "You don't have to worry about work; family and other things pass you by. You don't have any other problems, but you have one big one . . . then you can put up a fight. You no longer bother about anything except your illness. You've only one aim in life, suddenly, to get better."

Per contra, inactivity is filled by the struggle against illness, and by this very fact becomes tolerable. "You spend so much energy in this struggle of the organism to recover that you suffer less on account of your inactivity."

The loss of social role here brings neither complete emptiness nor annihilation. A woman patient with cancer who had nevertheless resumed a normal life expresses the idea that the patient's struggle takes the place of the healthy person's occupation, to such a degree that the two are incompatible: "Illness is an occupation, now I know it's an occupation. Only, I'd say that for me, it's more of an occupation when I can put up a fight against my illness. Now I no longer fight because I'm working, I haven't the time."

The conception of illness as an occupation includes two points which seem to represent the basic factors in the struggle against illness.
1. The patient no doubt fears his illness, but he always accepts it. Unlike the patient confronted with destructive illness, he does not feel that he has any possibility of denying it: it is there. A female patient says: "I'm terribly afraid of illness, I hate illness . . . but you know, as far as I'm concerned, it's rather like having a double with me now, I've got to accept it, I can't get rid of it." We find an accident described in the same way. Here also, denial is impossible. "It's an unpleasant ordeal, to be obliged to remain without moving for several months, but you just have to put up with the inevitable." To accept one's illness or one's accident is also to accept the amount of time it takes up in one's life. Here we can see the contrast with "destructive illness". Illness is a period to get through which must be regarded as such, "Since I knew it would be very long, I allowed a period of time in my life for it, and, for a certain length of time, I was ready for anything."

Sometimes we find it expressed as the need to establish oneself in one's illness. "The disease becomes established in you and you establish yourself in the disease. You've got to get right into the disease, like getting into a hole."
2. Constrained to accept his illness—it thereby shows its power— the patient nevertheless has over his illness a kind of power which originates in the very need to accept. This power has various degrees, or successively more active forms. First, one endures and in fact believes that no illness or pain is unendurable. "Healthy people certainly imagine that it's more difficult to endure. You quite often hear people saying, 'I could never endure that.' This is meaningless because, from

the moment that you put up with things, you just have to put up with them . . . You have to take whatever comes, and finally, you finish up putting up with almost everything, with everything." We can feel the value aspect associated with this endurance. "To put up with" may be already synonymous with "to overcome". It is also said that someone can adjust to his illness, live with the limitations which in particular it imposes. The victim of the accident to whom we have already referred says: "I lost an eye and, obviously, I'll always be afraid of having an accident which deprives me of the other one. I can't say I contemplate it with equanimity, but I think you can manage to regain your equilibrium . . . I think I'd adjust almost as well."

Illness and infirmity are then compared to a social situation which makes the same kind of demands on the individual. "Man establishes himself in his infirmity just as he adjusts to more or less any social situation he finds himself in . . . that is, you cut your losses, you adjust to the situation, you save what you can of what's left . . . it makes for permanent discomfort, but you get used to permanent discomfort . . . you develop your other organs and you make out."

Finally—and this appears connected with his endurance—the patient can, through his fight, participate in his cure. He hastens or facilitates it. This orientation towards cure is one of the distinguishing features of this conception. "I think you have a quite extraordinary desire to live . . . you have such a desire to recover that morally and psychologically you help your organism to recover."

The expression "to recover" recurs repeatedly among subjects. We have here a particular case of the problem of the participation of the person in his illness. So far, we have seen people maintaining that the rejection of illness might contribute to checking it (destructive illness) or that the hankering after it might facilitate its development (illness as a liberator). In the present case, we have people accepting the presence of illness without wishing for it. Psychological factors have an especially important role here, but at a different level. They are operative in the fight for cure.

On the other hand, there is scarcely any attempt to define the nature of this psychological struggle or this beneficial power of the "mind" or the "will". As we have already several times observed (cf. the analysis of the notions of "unhealthy" and of "equilibrium"), the intensity of belief obscures the lack of clarity of the belief itself.

In "illness as an occupation", special attention is given to certain characteristics of the states, and the notions of health and illness themselves are viewed in a special way.

The perception of physical phenomena and their consequent integration in the concept of illness is most complete in this conception of illness. Pain, fatigue and even temperature, here more than in the other conceptions, form part of the picture of illness and serve to define it. There is nothing surprising about this. The conception of "destructive illness" views illness only in terms of its consequences such as the loss of social role. It rejects knowledge of the physical condition just as it also rejects the state of illness itself. In the case of "illness as an occupation", on the contrary, the action and struggle presuppose knowledge. The attack is therefore more perceived in its physical aspects.

At the same time, the perception of illness is also more differentiated. Instead of viewing it as a global phenomenon (as in destructive illness) or restricting themselves to a few kinds of illness (illness as a liberator), these informants use many qualifications, make more distinctions,[1] and note fine shades of difference in the nature and type of illness.

One view of health is crucial here: that of the "reserve of health". In qualitative terms, we may note the very great importance which is attributed to it. "I had an incredible reserve of health which enabled me to respond to everything."

The importance attributed to the "reserve of health" may be partly the sign of greater participation—which would go with acceptance—of the individual in his own condition. It indicates that he feels himself concerned in his body. But most importantly, the reserve of health is the main factor in resistance to illness. We find again here the main theme of the conception. On the one hand, acceptance is accompanied by a finer perception of the physical attack itself—the illness is particularly observed and particularly important on the physical level. On the other hand, the fight the individual puts up and his power appear on two levels: on the psychological level in the form of the "mind" and the "will", and on the physical level in the form of the "reserve of health".

Those who tend to the "illness as an occupation" view also give most attention to the behaviour of the invalid, and refer to every aspect of it. Going to the doctor, which has the three-fold aim of diagnosis, therapy

[1] See chapter 6, analysis of types of illness. Each subject distinguishes, on average, four types of illness or affliction, compared with two on average for the other two conceptions. The most frequently made distinctions are those between serious and mild illness, between illness and accident, and lastly between painful and painless illness.

and prevention, is the crucial factor; it unambiguously defines the sick role. But it goes together with the personal and above all psychological struggle of the patient. It is believed that it is because of the "mental factor", the will, that the care and the attention of the doctor will be effective. "There's the principle, 'God helps those who help themselves'; you have to get to work on your own behalf; all those who have been ill say the same, it's certain that you cling to life . . . in an illness, I think that the person's mental attitude and his reactions are very important and make the doctor's job easier."

Relations with the doctor are thus conceived as a form of cooperation or exchange. In the extreme case, the sick role appears as just as active a role as the doctor's, almost on an equal footing. Strict, passive obedience is rejected in favour of a more symmetrical relationship. "The doctor does what he can, but the patient has to put in something of his own, so that there is a kind of collaboration between the patient and doctor. The doctor must help the patient to recover and give him medicines appropriate for his illness . . . but on his side, the patient must make a mental effort and discipline himself."

This desire for a kind of exchange can also be seen in respect of information. "To know", for the patient, is to possess one of the things necessary for his mental effort and fight. "First of all, I want to be told the truth . . . you can be more effective if you know just what's the matter with you, and what you are fighting against."

But this also involves making certain demands on the doctor, in return for the compliance and confidence which he demands of you. "I'd have no hesitation in going to competent doctors in order to get better health, and I'd have complete confidence in them, but I wouldn't want them to hide my condition from me and I'd want them to tell me frankly what was wrong."

As is very clearly suggested, "to know" is to be involved in the situation in the same way as the doctor, on an equal footing. "The doctors began by saying, 'Don't worry'. I said: 'Yes, all right, but I want to know. I don't want people to put me off any more; I want to know what they're doing to me. I'm not a fool'."

The picture of the patient, based on the activity aspect, on his participation in being ill, thus loses its dramatic character. Illness is still a trial, but it is not, in itself, a threat of annihilation. Those who have had experience of serious illness or accident reckon that one can "live with" illness. They accept that anxiety and fear have a place in this experience.

The female cancer patient already referred to remarks: "I think I can live with it, and, you know, I don't have a bad life." She continues: "You know, I'm scared just the same, everybody is; but you know, you live with it; I think everybody who has something wrong with him lives with his ailment."

Again, as far as the mood or affective state of the patient is concerned, the picture is no longer the agonizing picture of destructive illness. This point was made by one of our subjects: "I've noticed that there are quite a few people who aren't so demoralized in the face of illness as you might think . . . they find themselves facing a quite urgent problem. In this situation, they often show a tremendous energy which enables them to get over it and which is almost a source of satisfaction."

The experience of illness may lose the exceptional character and the beneficial quality which the notion of "illness as a liberator" attributes to it. It may, nevertheless, like any other experience which makes demands on energy and will-power, have aspects beneficial for the personality. Thus, it may be thought that the person comes out of an illness "stronger". "You are stronger in the sense that when you have experience of something, you have more self confidence. Anyone who has had to make efforts to endure suffering is less likely to let himself go . . . the individual is mentally more resistant."

But there is a kind of continuity between the situation and the personality of the healthy person and the situation and personality of the sick person. The sick person may be "stronger" than before but he remains himself. The process of "strengthening" involves neither depersonalization nor transformation.

Similarly, relations with others are not radically transformed. In spite of all obstacles, communication is maintained. The patient does not feel himself wholly isolated from healthy people. "You still retain your connection with the outside world through your friends, who carry on normal activities."

There is special emphasis on the help which his associates can provide for the patient in his struggle. For example, one of our subjects said: "Their attachment acted just like a tonic. I'm sure that the presence of people you're attached to, and all the manifestations of affection and tenderness they give you, help you in the most material and concrete way."

But, in addition, new relations may be inaugurated—relations with other patients. The world of invalids is sometimes represented as an interdependent world in which, for example, there may be stimulation by others. A patient may want to be an example for other patients. "I very much wanted to get better because I wanted to show the others that you could get better."

The patient sees himself as one among others. "You say to yourself, 'I'm an invalid, just like my neighbour, who has chronic bronchitis'." For our subjects, to be an invalid is to belong in a social category like other social categories. The world of invalids is a socialized world.

The identity of invalid and healthy person, and the socialized nature of both illness and health are, indeed, the two crucial aspects of this conception. Any general view of "illness as an occupation" would have to include the following aspects.

1. The preservation of the social values of health within illness. Activity, energy and will define the invalid and illness just as they define the healthy person and health.

2. Illness is a learning situation; the invalid learns to struggle and becomes "stronger" and the result of this process of learning can also be used when the patient is restored to health.

3. Cure is the normal outcome of illness: the invalid is "occupied with getting cured". Illness represents essentially the stage and the behaviour by which, after a physical attack, cure is achieved. It is a "time to get through" and therefore takes its place along with the "socialized time" of health.

4. In the case of chronic illness, adjustment is possible. The individual creates a new form of life for himself, with limitations, agreed, but also with compensations and with new interests.

The invalid is therefore not defined by values and a personality basically different from those of the healthy person. Similarly, illness remains, like health, a socialized situation.

Illness and health are not two entirely different kinds of thing. They both form part of a single whole. Life includes both health and illness within its scope. Again, society does not reject the invalid nor dissociate itself from the world of invalids. The consequence of this view is that there can be no real deviance in illness or in the invalid. The behaviour of the invalid is the process by which he not only responds to physical attack but also asserts the enduring nature of his belongingness to society.

9

The Invalid and his Identity

"Destructive illness", "illness as a liberator" and "illness as an occupation" all include attitudes and behaviour which have been described in the sociological literature. Various authors have referred to the "denial" of illness. Lederer (1952), for example, regards this as the first stage of reaction to illness. Denial may further be not only by the patient himself, but also by his associates. A number of studies (see, for example, Schwartz, 1957; Yarrow *et al.*, 1960) describe the process; for example, the "minimization" of symptoms or the tendency to "normalize" the behaviour of the mental patient by selective perception and recourse to rational explanations.

Other studies relate the refusal of special measures to different kinds or personal attitude and social values. Thus for Phillips (1965), "resistance to taking the sick role" is associated with assertions of the subject's autonomy. Goldstein and Eichhorn (1961) considered resistance to special measures, mistrust of the doctor, and belief in the possibility of controlling one's health personally through one's will, to be traits characteristic of the traditional Protestant ideology—losing ground in American society—dominated by individualism and asceticism with the central value of devotion to work.

These studies emphasize the high value placed on the activity and autonomy of the healthy person which we have noted as characterizing the view of illness that we have called "destructive illness".

Similarly, notions of "illness as a liberator", based on data supplied by the subjects themselves and not the observer, fit in with the analyses which find illness to represent a form of escape mechanism, on the basis of the egocentrism and introversion of the invalid, and the restriction of his interest in the outside world (see, for example, Barker *et al.*, 1953; Balint 1957).

Finally, the view of "illness as an occupation" presents the picture of an active patient, cooperating with the doctor, using in the struggle for cure all the energy freed by the removal of social obligations. Here we have the characteristics of the "sick role" as defined by Parsons; the patient is exempted from responsibilities and is entitled to help, but he must want to be cured and take an active part in the therapeutic process if he is to be regarded as satisfying the demands of society.

There is also considerable agreement with some empirical studies of Parsonian inspiration. In a study of seriously ill patients who had experimental therapy in hospital, Fox (1959) shows that acceptance and an active attitude, a desire for information, mutual stimulation by members of the group and cooperation with doctors are of primary importance in the attitudes and behaviour of patients. Our subjects present the same picture.

Thus, observers find themselves in essential agreement with those immediately involved. This again suggests the common ground between the man in the street and the sociologist. But in our view, the principal interest of an examination of the norms of illness behaviour does not lie in looking at content.

What seem to us more important are the possibilities which such a study offers of achieving a comprehensive understanding of the different modes of response to illness. While each theoretical approach, e.g. psychoanalytical theory and its concern with the notion of avoidance in illness, or Parsonian theory, emphasizes one kind of response, one kind of behaviour distinct from others, our study enables these different kinds of response to be brought together. The three conceptions of illness have, in fact, a common thread, to which we have drawn attention throughout: the relations of the individual with society.

In the case of "destructive illness", the person finds self-definition, self-expression and achievement in social participation. Illness which brings social exclusion cannot but be experienced as annihilation; and so one is obliged to deny it.

In the case of "illness as a liberator", on the other hand, the release from social obligations represents for the individual a liberation which enables him to find complete fulfilment. The element of avoidance in illness, or at least its temptation, takes the place of denial.

The third conception (of "illness as an occupation") differs from both the others—which are diametrically opposed—in that it does not accept the equating of illness and social exclusion. The invalid's struggle guarantees him the maintenance of his integration in society.

Each notion represents a specific view of illness, each oriented by different conceptions of the relations of the individual to society. The relation of individual to society finds a crucial expression in the notion of activity–inactivity. According to whether social activity is perceived as maintained or undermined, according to whether it does or does not represent a value for the person, the person sees himself confronted by a series of alternatives which determine the meaning of his experience. These are concerned, as we have seen, with social participation, with life or death. Is illness identified with death—perhaps physical but more often social—or is it a form of life? These alternatives also have to do with his identity. "Who am I?" the invalid asks. "Am I the same or not? How am I transformed?"

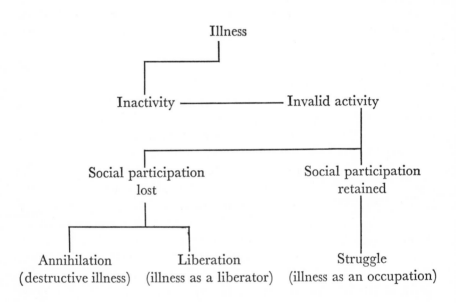

Parallel to this manipulation of the meaning accorded to phenomena and to different evaluations of them, each conception involves a different kind of cognitive organization. Each conception involves a different picture. Thus, in "destructive illness", the misunderstanding of physical phenomena, the tendency to extend the notion of health and to restrict that of illness seem closely associated with the tendency to deny illness. In "illness as an occupation", on the other hand, the finer appreciation of the physical aspects and the more differentiated perception of different kinds of ailment seem to be related to the patient's struggle. In "illness as a liberator", it is most frequently because of the concentration upon certain kinds of illness—benign, short and painless—that illness appears to have lost its destructive nature.

These are relatively crude distinctions. They do, however, indicate that each conception can be regarded as giving a comprehensive view of the phenomena of health and illness. Each model of behaviour and each type of response can therefore be regarded in terms of its meaning for the individual and the way he organizes it.

Our viewpoint is different from those in which the invalid is confronted with a norm outside himself, in which emphasis is placed on the regression of the invalid compared with the healthy person, and in which attention is directed towards the "magical" nature of his behaviour—denial of illness[1] or recourse to quack doctors (see the article by Cobb (1958) on the question of recourse to quacks), for instance—compared with the rationality assumed to be shown by acceptance of medical directions. From the point of view of the individual, the three conceptions of illness would appear to represent three coherent strategies in relation to somewhat different ends which may be defined in the following way: "not to be ill" in the case of destructive illness; "to be ill" in the case of illness as a liberator; and "to be a good patient", i.e. try to get well, in the case of illness as an occupation. In the case of each one of these, a different kind of equilibrium becomes established for the relation of the sick or healthy individual to society, and for the relation of the individual in society to health and to illness.

In this respect, the present approach would seem to be complementary to that of Parsons. Parsons' analysis does seem relevant if one takes the point of view of society, but if one takes the point of view of the individual patient in society, it seems less applicable. Is illness as a form of deviance really experienced as such? What does it mean for the individual who is experiencing it? It would appear that there may be several answers to this question where Parsons has allowed only one.

In "destructive illness", the social norms which require health and activity are completely internalized. The individual in fact perceives the situation of being ill as a form of deviance which threatens his

---

[1] A number of authors, e.g. Parsons (1951), Valabrega (1962), regard denial of illness as having the quality of "magic". On the other hand, Clausen (1959) attributes a positive function to it, that of facilitating the resumption of normal activities.

F

self concept and identity. In this case, the sick role, which would canalize his deviance, cannot emerge. When he internalizes the point of view of society, the individual refuses to accept himself as deviant. The only kind of control possible to him is not a form of social control, through the action of his associates and doctor and through conformity to their expectations, but an individual kind of control in the shape of the persistence of the role of healthy person. When that is not possible, the individual relapses into passivity and his identity cannot be restored.

In "illness as a liberator", on the other hand, the identity of the person asserts itself through the deviance of illness. It is by distinguishing himself from others and from himself when well that the individual achieves a fully satisfying conception of himself. He asserts the non-conforming aspect of illness.

Finally, in "illness as an occupation", the problem is set in different terms. As we have indicated, the behaviour of the invalid and his struggle are comprised in the sick role as defined by Parsons; social control is in command. The significance of patient behaviour seems to be to prevent illness from being experienced as deviance. Illness is experienced in terms of the setting up of new norms, and of a special but persistent form of social integration. Illness remains a socially recognized condition. The individual retains his identity and remains the same in illness as in health.

Parsons' analysis emphasizes the point of view of society, describes the nature of social demands and thereby presents a model of a social system in equilibrium. Patient and doctor have complementary relations and the patient assumes a role which leads to cure and to social re-integration. Our own analysis suggests that for the individual with his two-fold relationship to illness and to society, there may be more than one solution, and that the perception of deviance and the controls which govern it may be related in more than one way.

The concepts of conformity and deviance, in which the demands of society find expression, here seem to be less important than that of identity which, through deviance and conformity, reflects the subject's own experience. Two aspects are involved. Subjects seek to understand the nature of their identity, that is their social identity, the image of themselves as they appear to others and as expressed in their social role and conformity, or identity as the conception of themselves which asserts itself in non-conformity and finds expression in withdrawal from society. Secondly, they question themselves about the enduring quality of their identity. Is there a self-identity which persists throughout both illness and health?

Each of the three conceptions of illness can be regarded from the point of view of these two aspects of the self concept—as more or less defined by social participation, or as social identity on the one hand, and as more or less liable to reorganization from health to illness, on the other.

The nature of our data do not allow us to study the relations of these conceptions of illness and of these norms of behaviour to actual behaviour itself. However, two relevant points may be made.

1. Of the different conceptions of illness, are there any which, in the view of our informants, seem to correspond to actual experience of illness, while others exist only on the representational level and involve imaginary rather than actual experience? In fact, the notion of "illness as an occupation" seems to be associated with present experience of illness and of severe illness in the past. (Included in the 17 cases on which the analysis is based there were six people who were ill at the time of the interview and seven who had in the past had experience of serious illness.) This is less frequently so for "destructive illness", while, of those who described illness as a "liberator", not one was currently ill and only one said he had had a serious illness. The conception of illness as an occupation is therefore most frequent among "the ill". That of illness as a liberator occurs especially among the "healthy" and seems to express weariness with social obligations and the temptation offered by illness rather than the actual experience. According to numerous studies, however, illness can represent avoidance behaviour, motivated in effect by its liberating character. We may suppose that, in invalids, this kind of genuinely deviant behaviour is, by reason of its very deviant nature, less readily integrated into an organized representation. In this case, we may venture the hypothesis of a possible disagreement between behaviour and representation. In the case of "illness as an occupation", if this accurately reflects, as we believe it does, experience of illness, only future studies directed at observation of actual behaviour would enable us to test the hypothesis of an agreement between the conception of "illness as an occupation" and the behaviour of struggle against illness.

2. We may inquire precisely what role is played by the representation in the genesis of behaviour and its development and thus in the dynamics of the response to illness. The different conceptions, especially those of

"destructive illness" and "illness as an occupation" seem to correspond to different stages of illness. Reflection on the nature of "destructive illness", together with the supporting examination of the literature, suggests that primarily it operates at the beginning of the illness and may appear as an immediate perception of reality, from which will originate the processes of rejection. "Illness as an occupation", on the other hand, presupposes the elapse of some period of time during which the subject has "learned the trade of patient". It should be regarded less as a genetic factor and more as an *a posteriori* notion in which the individual rationalizes his experience and organizes at the level of thought, behaviour which has developed progressively from the initial refusal to the acceptance of illness. The problem now becomes one of the change from one mode of response to the other, from destructive illness to illness as an occupation, from denial to acceptance. The literature of sociology provides no answer to this problem of the dynamics of the response to illness. Response to illness is most frequently dealt with chronologically by a description of the different kinds of behaviour of the patient as these succeed one another. The patient passes from rejection to acceptance, or the sick role, as Parsons puts it, channels the patient's tendencies to avoidance. But there is no explanatory account of this change and development.

It is scarcely possible in the present study to attempt an interpretation in this area. We must be satisfied simply to emphasize that what is involved is not just a change but a real reorganization of the subject's identity involving the individual, his illness and society.

Activity (or inactivity) plays an essential part therein. Thus, in the change from destructive illness to illness as an occupation, after a stage in which illness, because of the inactivity it involves, appears as a threat to social identity and as annihilation and therefore induces denial, reorganization takes place when the recourse to special attention is seen no longer as a failure of the attitude of denial but as a new activity which restores to the individual a positive role and a conception of a socialized self. Illness then ceases to be a form of deviance. At this point, in addition to the intrinsic requirements of the situation, social pressures also come to bear on the individual to facilitate this reorganization and we should no doubt go more deeply into the relations between these factors. On the other hand, when action appears as impossible or useless, the threat of annihilation persists and the individual clings to unyielding denial or gives way to passivity. An examination of certain "mixed cases"—where the individual vacillates between more than one conception of illness—indicates that the individual vacillates between denial and acceptance as a function of whether or not he thinks he can "do anything".

The most complex case is that in which the individual, by escaping into illness, creates a very satisfying self picture. How can the individual be brought to give up this conception and return to a more conforming kind of integration into society? How can activity in the form of the patient's struggle fulfil a positive function? If, as Parsons maintains, social pressures are powerful, it may nevertheless be the case that the nature of the illness and in particular its seriousness may play a vital part. In the face of an illness seen as physically threatening, the privileges and satisfactions which the illness brings most frequently become of secondary importance. The struggle, when it is possible, takes over. Several cases show the following pattern: while the subjects value the avoidance made possible by illness seen as a liberating force when it is relatively benign, they assert the necessity of struggle and concomitantly the positive role of social integration when the illness is serious.

All these issues remain open. Parsonian analysis indicates that, in order to satisfy social requirements, the individual must substitute the aim of "being a good patient" for "not being ill" or "being ill". We do not know how this substitution comes about. What is required is a more detailed study of the various forms of relation between social pressures, the demands of the situation and the individual's own notions, based on observation of actual behaviour.

Conclusion

Throughout the present study, we have been concerned to observe how the individual's picture of health and illness develops. This picture does not reflect the totality of his knowledge, nor does it always reflect his actual behaviour. It was not our intention to consider such aspects, but rather to see how the individual organizes his knowledge into a meaningful picture and how he himself interprets his behaviour. We have seen how the individual gives meaning to and organizes reality and his own experience by the selective perception, sometimes schematizing and sometimes distorting, which he applies to these aspects of his life. We do not therefore claim to be offering an analysis of illness

behaviour (or of the health behaviour of the healthy person); our
study has rather followed a complementary approach to the study of
these forms of behaviour by attempting to cast light on the subject's
own point of view.

Similarly, we have made no attempt to study the public's "information" or understanding of medical knowledge—its content or progress—
but have been concerned with the individual's conception of reality
without attempting to relate this to norms extrinsic to that conception.
In the course of our observations, we attached relatively little importance to information for its own sake, or to possible instances of
convergence of popular and medical notions, although some authors
have noted that such convergence proceeds in both directions, that is
from specialist to layman and from layman to specialist; it has been
emphasized (see, for example, Gourevitch, 1964; Allendy, 1944) that
the doctor is himself a layman, especially when he is ill. We have
been concerned rather to understand the frame of reference within
which such information is organized. What we examined was the idiom
in which phenomena were interpreted, communicated and grasped.

One point soon becomes clear: the language of illness is not a
language of the body. While right through the study we can see the
frequency of language and descriptions involving the state of mind and
behaviour of the patient, there is nothing about the body itself. The
body, the actual organic condition, gets forgotten and lost between
illness as the result of the "way of life", and the behaviour of the patient.
Images and notions relevant to normal bodily functioning are rare and
feeble; even more rare are images and notions designed to express
organic pathology and the outbreak of illness. Resistance, the only
function attributed to it, is regarded as the overall resistance of a more
or less solid material body rather than in terms of the interaction and
complex adjustive mechanisms of a real organism. (From this point of
view, we might go beyond the poverty of these images of the body—
which in themselves form a deserving object of study—and ask what
the public's image of life is and how many people think of the nature
of the living.)

Moreover, while for our subjects the person and behaviour of the invalid are organized in ordered wholes which we have described as specific conceptions of illness and the invalid (see chapter 8)—though here
they have a synthesizing and coordinating function—physical phenomena, especially physical signs, are thought of separately, each with a

localizing function, which in any case is most often misleading (see chapter 6, analysis of the physical signs of illness) and not as related to a total conception. They are not organized into any ordered system, but constitute unreliable additional cues which must be assimilated to another whole and to a different language, that of the behaviour and personality of the patient, before they can be seen as significant.

Certainly, in our society there is a group which occupies a special position in regard to everything concerning the body, namely doctors.[1] Gourevitch emphasizes that patients describe bodily symptoms in localizing terms. For him (1964), the patient's notions are "such as to localize as much as possible the functions and their weaknesses" (Gourevitch, 1964, p. 13). He adds: "These localising notions which are clearly present in popular pathology and which are very ready to refer to an internal organ by way of diagnosis ("it's my liver") are simply the exaggeration of a genuinely medical tendency." (1964, p. 14.) He nevertheless opposes to these popular notions the medical way of thinking which operates in diagnosis: for the doctor, the illness is understood as a "group of symptoms", a whole made up of related signs, coordinated within the framework of a pathological process. The contradiction between a conception concerned with localization and analysis on the one hand, and a conception concerned with coordination and synthesis on the other is one of the reasons for the difficulty of communication between doctor and patient. (It may further be emphasized that the doctor often tends to communicate only as little information as possible to the patient and his family, and therefore makes scarcely any attempt to develop the patient's notions—see Davis, 1960.)

This notion of localization, which tries to make a single organ correspond to each sign, would appear to be closely associated with the poverty of body language—a language where sentences and syntax are ignored and there are only nouns. The individual supplies the doctor with, or obtains from him, the name of an organ, just as he supplies or obtains the name of an illness. Just as for the child, the stage of the "word-phrase" represents the first, crudest and most unorganized stage of language, so for the patient, the juxtaposing of the name of an organ

[1] This might perhaps be the reason for the scarcity of images of the body in our inquiry—we were not "good" recipients. However, although the individual may rarely speak of his body except to the doctor, he spoke freely to us about his illness; it is thus clear that one does not need to use the language of the body in order to talk about illness.

and the name of an illness represents the elementary use, the only use he can grasp, of the organic language of illness.

But the organic or physical can find expression in a different language —not the language of the interior world which is the body, but the language of relation to the outside world, more precisely to the "socialized" outside world. The language of health and illness is structured by the relation of the individual to others and to society.

We have repeatedly shown the role of the relation between the individual and society, the true frame of reference of the representation, but return to this point once again to emphasize the integrating function of the relation. From this point of view the representation develops on three levels: that of experience itself, that of the conceptions which make sense of it and that of the norms of behaviour deriving from it.

Experience takes meaning, at both the physical and psychosocial levels, in terms of the relations of the individual to society. Similarly, the very ideas of health and illness become organized to express experience. A language of health and illness is elaborated which is interwoven with the language of the relations of the individual to society. Activity (or inactivity) and the social participation (or exclusion) which gives the individual's experience meaning are also the notions used to define the invalid and the healthy person and to distinguish between health and illness. In both cases, the "working" of experience and information, the cognitive organization of phenomena, is oriented by these organizing social values. It leads to a norm of the healthy person and of the invalid—the individual as active or inactive in society—and thus provides a means of overcoming the uncertainty of the inexpressible physical aspect. At a different level, it also determines norms of behaviour for the healthy person and the sick person— denial of illness and maintenance of social activity, or acceptance and the invalid's struggle, for example—which are norms of behaviour of the individual in society. The uncertainty which has to be overcome is then that of the social identity of the subject, threatened by illness.

In this reciprocal articulation of different levels of psychosocial phenomena—cognitive organization of a social object and elaboration of norms of behaviour—which are usually studied separately, lies, in our view, one of the main interests of a study of representations. The articulation appears most clearly in the notion of activity–inactivity. Of primary importance because of this unifying role on the cognitive level, this notion would also appear to have another essential function, that of anchorage in the development of the representation. Such a process, according to Moscovici, enables us to take account of the formation of "a network of meanings round the central image of the social representation" and to grasp how the representation can become a "framework of interpretation mediating between the individual and his world". Around the notion of activity–inactivity, in fact, crystallizes the totality of meanings affecting the experience of illness, as these meanings are constituted in social life. Giving up activity becomes the sign of illness. But reciprocally, the representation itself acquires a function. Through it, by refusal or justification of the inactivity of the invalid, the subject's attempt to relate himself to society as a whole finds expression. The notions of health and illness are thus expressed and grasped on the cognitive level in a language of the relations of the individual to society.

In health, this relation is unique. It expresses and extends the individual by binding him to society. In the image of illness, on the other hand, we find reflected the coexistence of an illness external to the individual and of his own illness behaviour. The individual interprets illness as a product of, and imposed upon him by, the way of life; he nevertheless expresses himself and locates himself in society through illness behaviour.[1] The richness and complexity of the image of illness reside in, and are to be understood in terms of, this duality and this two-fold movement—constraint of society on the individual and action and adjustment of the individual in society.

For the individual, to interpret illness is to impute its genesis to a provoking society. In two senses, illness is conceived as "illness of the society". Its distribution is social. Every society, and our own in particular, has "its illnesses"; the "illnesses of modern life" are, for our subjects, the prevalent expressions of this fact. It is also social by its very nature; the intrusion of the way of life and social constraint are perceived as illness present or future.

Such a representation suggests primitive notions according to which the breaking of contact with the group and conflict with or exclusion from the collectivity may be sufficient to cause death, in the absence of any physical disorder (and frequently do in fact cause death). Mauss has given the following account of such phenomena: "[The individual

---

[1] Moscovici (1961), p. 336. We are concerned here with his analysis of the notion of anchorage. This is very different from the usual use of the term in social psychology.

dies because he] believes himself to be solely for definite collective causes, in a state near to death. This state generally coincides with a rupture of communion, whether by magic or as a result of wrongdoing, with the powers and sacred objects the presence of which normally affords him support."[1] (1950, p. 314.) These well-known facts, for which Cannon (1944) has supplied a physiological explanation, are, according to Mauss, rare or nonexistent in our society. But it is nevertheless the case that for us also, at least at the level of representations, a certain social state—the "external" relation of the individual to his way of life— leads to physical conflict and becomes embodied in it. Just as, according to Mauss, the primitive collectivity suggests the idea of death to the individual, so our society suggests the idea of illness to each of its members.

Through health and illness, we thus have access to the image of society and of its constraints, as the individual sees them. Absorbed in this image, illness takes on a new significance. For us as for primitive man, it is probably important that illness, even if it is regarded as "disorder", should not be a matter of chance, but should be significant even as a "disorder". It encompasses and crystallizes social constraint; the invalid then finds himself relieved of all responsibility for the start of his condition.

It is certain that these images which so obviously relieve the individual of any blame cannot but represent a defence against a latent feeling of guilt. Doubtless the individual only asserts with such vehemence that illness comes from "the other" because he is afraid that it may indeed have its source in himself. But whether it comes from himself—whether it is "his own fault"—or whether it comes as a threat from without, in interpreting "without"—society—as pathogenic, in refusing to be the origin of illness, the individual responds to the threat and transforms his possible responsibility into an accusation, making the invalid the victim who exemplifies the forces bearing upon us. Thereby, the invalid may indeed rediscover a symbolic function in society. The question of the social status of the invalid has been raised; it has been interpreted as that of a deviant, and also in terms of attitudes towards him, whether of rejection or of support. We have taken a more general view and have asked what the invalid's symbolic function is. This

[1] The study by Whiteman and Lukoff (1965) shows by use of the semantic differential that the infirm and the sick are perceived differently from (less negatively than) the corresponding illness or infirmity. This seems to confirm our distinction between illness regarded as an "object", a threat from without, and the personality of the sick person.

may provide a new perspective for the study of the status of the invalid and of attitudes towards him.

If the individual sets himself in opposition to society and defends himself against it by asserting his lack of responsibility for his illness, and if he expresses his dissatisfaction with the constraints of society, he nevertheless also expresses its values, and locates himself and defines himself within it; by health, first of all the activity of the healthy person, a fundamental value as indicated by the representation, appears in its function of structuring the social identity of the subject.

As far as illness is concerned, Bastide emphasizes that we define mental illness by reference to an ideology of "producers": "Deviance is defined by our modes of production and insanity is consequently first and foremost a form of unproductivity." (1965, p. 249.) It is indeed thus, as a form of unproductivity, that the individual perceives illness in general; it is in relation to the values of activity and production that we understand the norms of illness behaviour and the different modes of response to the external object which illness in the first instance is. The individual will accept the illness as his own and will accept himself as an invalid if, by fighting, he can cooperate in a new mode of production. He produces his cure and thereby re-enters society. Illness is viewed as a job. He may, on the other hand, choose, by avoiding social constraints, to produce nothing but himself in illness. This is the undoubtedly and fundamentally anti-conformist choice in "illness as a liberator".

Health and illness, individual and society are thus always associated by various but indissoluble ties. Although a number of studies have dealt with the attitudes and behaviour of invalids or of healthy people towards invalids, the present study illustrates *in vivo* the development of the meaning of illness for the individual in relation to both illness and society. A unitary and dynamic approach to behaviour seems possible from this point of view, and ought to be pursued.

Health and illness thus appear as a mode of interpretation of society by the individual, and as a mode of relation of the individual to society. We have tried to describe health and illness under this double aspect. In attempting this task we have been aware of uncertainties, and have at times done no more than make a beginning. Our choice of primarily descriptive method undoubtedly imposed limitations. Such a method is well suited for locating problems, but more rarely for resolving them. But, after this first approach, which appeared indispensable, for it can be postulated that progress in theory is often inseparable from progress in the description of phenomena, it becomes possible to follow up the investigation with other methods and more limited objectives. We do, however, hope that the present study has in places shown how the relation to a social object becomes structured in the course of relations with others and thus with society; and how relations with others and with society become structured in the course of relation to the social object. This would appear to be a proper object of psychosocial research.

Appendix 1

The interview guide was composed of the following themes.

1. Definitions and classifications of illness. What distinctions do people make? How are different states delimited and by what signs?
2. Norms with regard to health and illness. What occurs most frequently? What appears as most normal?
3. The principal cause of illness.
4. The role of pain and death in relation to illness.
5. The importance of illness for the individual and for his personality.
6. The behaviour found in illness (in the case of illness of the subject and of illness of other people).
7. What illnesses are feared?
8. The factors important for health.
9. The importance of health for the individual and for personality.
10. Health behaviour.
11. Is it possible to imagine a world in which there would be no illness, a world without any illness?

Appendix 2

The extracts from the interviews which we give here are intended to give the reader some appreciation of the data which will be less fractionated than any that may be gained from reading the quotations in the text.

We have selected three interviews to illustrate the three conceptions of "destructive illness", "illness as a liberator" and "illness as an occupation". (Only short extracts are given. Because of the length of the actual interviews (25 to 50 pages) it was impossible to include even one in its entirety.)

Destructive illness

Mme G, 33 years of age

"The first threat to my health I've ever had was this year; in fact, I've never had to go to bed since I was married and have had the children, and I've always had good health. I soon get better from 'flu' or a sore throat, I try to stop it at the outset, I resist the attack and don't go to bed. This winter, I had to stay in bed for three weeks. The only thing I was thinking of, and the only thing my husband was thinking of was to get myself on my feet again as soon as possible so as to resume a normal life. I'm bound to say that it shakes me when I'm just going along and I come across people who say, 'My child is ill, he's been having treatment for three months, I have so and so and my oldest son has ever so many things wrong with him and my husband has such and such.' I'm overwhelmed by anything like that, I can't contemplate such a thing.

". . . No, I can't believe that that can happen all of a sudden in a family . . . I think that, whatever, when people talk to you about illness,

142

they accept this as a matter of fact. It seems to me that I just don't accept the fact of being ill; you know, it's something that has to be settled very quickly, I don't readily accept it when I'm ill. I know that this winter, I got really ill, for a couple of days, I thought I'd have to go to hospital for an operation; well, half an hour after the doctor had left, I said to myself, 'Well, I won't have that, I won't go.' Well, it may be silly, because I think that if the attention and treatment I had hadn't been enough, I'd have had to have an operation just the same. But I was sure, from the beginning, that I was going to get better quickly. And then when the doctor came the second day and said, 'Good, well now, I don't think we need an operation', I responded rapidly because here, it was terrible, here, where you aren't used to being ill, you aren't ready for it. The children didn't know what they were doing in the house, my husband had ever so much to do and wasn't ever able to serve the meals as he wanted. In fact, it was a week of absolute chaos, and in spite of it all, I tried to get better straight away.

"Obviously, there are incurable diseases; just think of an attack of polio which puts you in a chair for the rest of your life, now I confess that's one of the rare diseases that really frightens me, because, in fact, that may be a matter of paralysis. You can't do anything about it, you just have to live like that. But how you would react to that, I don't know, I just don't see how . . . I have difficulty in imagining myself having a long illness . . . I think I'd have awful difficulty in accepting that kind of thing, I think I'd be in an awful taking . . . because I think of my life here, with my children and my husband. I think that, from the moment I was seriously ill, well, if there was really nothing could be done . . . that would be the end, family life wouldn't exist any more. I think that would be frightful; we would have to organize our life differently if I were to be in poor health, I'd no longer be able to do what I do with the children, I'd no longer be able to carry on as I do. Then, I'd be cut off from my family, life would have to go on without me . . . I wouldn't be able to play my part as I do now. I think anyone who is ill must be outside normal life . . . for children it's dreadful to have a mummy who is always tired, always ill, who isn't available any more . . . they can't count on their mother any more. During the month I was ill . . . well, life went on without me, I didn't feel any longer that I was taking part in it, I had the feeling of being outside it. . . .

"But you know, I think you have to try to do something, not to let yourself go . . . I happened to have friends who moaned about nothing.

I hate that, that gets me . . . and my husband thinks more or less like me. When he's ill, he hates to have anybody ask if he's feeling better, if he's still off colour. Again, people pass over that kind of thing, don't speak of it, avoid it . . . I can say of my husband that, when he's ill, he doesn't like anyone to see him taking medicines, he fixes it and makes sure he isn't seen, and I think that's important, it's something I do for the children too, when there are medicines or pills to be taken, so that it doesn't become an important thing in the house and everybody doesn't say, 'Right, it's now time.' That sort of thing creates a kind of state of illness, you are ill. I know people who complain about their illness and who think at three o'clock, I've got to take three pills, and at five o'clock two more. It's annoying, you do it, but . . . it mustn't become an established thing, you mustn't become established in your illness because, basically, when you're ill, you tend to lose the sense of your responsibilities. For myself, I know I would find it very tempting to take refuge in a 'no man's land'—'and now I can't do any more and other people can work it out'; and I think it's quite a serious thing if you get established in a state like that. Basically this is the kind of thing I was saying, this feeling of being marginal when you're ill, this must be a temporary thing which passes quickly, and normal life is resumed again . . . I feel that when you get established in an unhealthy state . . . well, you live in it. . . .

"Last week, I met a young woman I know whose husband is ill . . . He has disseminated sclerosis; he leads a sort of slow-motion life, his active life is virtually nil. I feel a sort of embarrassment with this family, it's the feeling that a person who is really ill, virtually incurable, is on the margin of life . . . well, it's an exceptional situation . . . it's completely destroyed their life. I think that if anything like that happened to us, if my husband found himself completely unable to get about, well, I think our life would be finished. I get that feeling when I see these people, that they've reached the end of their lives, while they are only 35. Perhaps for a writer, for example, for people who need quiet . . . you know, to be alone a bit to work out problems or ideas they have, they might even then achieve something; but I've the feeling that when an active life is hit by a serious illness, it's the end. I feel that a serious illness which prevents you from living normally, is a terminus, an end, I feel it's like death. . . .

"I don't see what can be done for him . . . nobody can help you to get better. If you can't endure this condition, if mentally you are really very much distressed, if you don't try any more, I don't think anyone can help you to try. What's terrible, basically, is that illness, I think, makes you really very much alone . . . you are really cut off from the world. When you are ill, you stay alone . . . there's scarcely any way of being helped . . . it undermines what you wanted to do and isolates you . . . And also, you can do nothing, that's what's awful . . . serious illness, well if you are there in your bed, afflicted with something which makes you half dead, you can't do anything, you just have to put up with it, that's what's terrible."

Illness as a liberator

Mlle R, 33 years of age

"I think illness is rather pleasant; I have rather pleasant memories of it, because when you're ill, you are an interesting person . . . at these times, it's important to live and not to be ill, while you aren't ill, that's not of any special importance. It's that above everything that matters, to put it bluntly, it's the kind of centre of interest that you become that is such a very pleasant thing. You have the feeling of being much more alive . . . everything takes on a more interesting light which is quite different from everyday life. . . .

"I think things are certainly new, become new, because of the presence or threat or possibility of death. I think everything becomes terribly fast, exciting and interesting when you're ill . . . I feel the days are at the same time both much longer and much shorter, time has a different tempo and passes differently. You have time to read and at the same time, you aren't quite sure what o'clock it is. You're relieved of everything that makes you waste time foolishly during life, only the important things still exist, among others, to be alive, it's as simple as that. You no longer want to see anybody except those who really matter and you are spared the others and there are no obligations except to yourself, that's to say, you get rid of everything that doesn't matter and you avoid what you daren't avoid in everyday life. You get the feeling of being much more alive, you have an exceptional and very pleasant freedom; it's a kind of renewal . . . Yes, it doesn't matter that you're stuck in bed, you have a wider range of possibilities open to you than when you have to work for your living and do a whole lot of things which basically are of no interest or value, either to you or to others. . . .

"I don't think people are very sincere when they say, 'I wish I could get out and do so and so.' Well, personally, I think I'd be less sincere than when I say, 'It would be wonderful to have a week or a fortnight to get one's bearings, to give up everything for a week or a fortnight and see where I got.' And I think that's a deeper and more genuine concern. You know, all children dream of being in danger of death to feel important and to see if their parents really love them. The condemnation to idleness and the justification of idleness by the necessity of rest is a very enriching experience, I think . . . it's the time when interpersonal relations are at their most crucial because there's a chance that they may disappear altogether; and that's when you can judge them best. You simply don't have normal relations with your doctor and your nurses. Your relations with them are more special, more definite, warmer, even a little sentimental . . . in relation to the doctor, you always want him to take a bit more care over you, to treat you a little differently from an ordinary patient and you always have the illusion that he is doing it. That's because all the other economic or social ties, and questions about usefulness, for example, the question 'Am I useful or not?' disappear when you're ill. Even under communist rule you have the right to be ill. You don't have the right to be useless to society, but once you're ill, you have the right to be ill . . . then, people don't make any demands on you except to get better. You don't ask anything of an invalid, you tell him to get better by having the patience to get better. . . .

"The number of people who tell you all the details of their illnesses . . . they need to talk about it because they need to justify themselves. If you haven't done anything in your life more interesting than have a stomach ulcer, you tell yourself that that at least is something interesting and worth talking about . . . it was the most outstanding experience of my life. Anyway, I think that, compared to serious illness, there are very few striking experiences in life. A really serious illness is like a first love affair, and I think more people would rather talk about their illness than about their first love. First love is less justifiable socially. Certainly, social security emphasizes this feeling because you get the impression that others are doing their bit to help you; or at least, your expenses are met by the community, therefore your general condition is of direct concern to society, since society pays for you, while society doesn't care a fig for your love anguish . . .

"I think illness has a lot of influence on people; it lets them be what they were before and couldn't be because of social circumstances . . . I think that if a person has intellectual interests, illness shows them. When he gets better, he'll become again somebody very ordinary and matter of fact. But, during the kind of holiday that illness provides, one can develop existing possibilities . . . afterwards, one becomes again a prisoner of the idea he has of himself or the idea others have of him or the situation he's in. . . .

"I think health depends a lot on the individual, on his wish for good health. I often have the feeling of sickening for something and I think that's a sign of the desire to be ill. The crucial factor is the power to get rid of the hankering after illness. If nobody wanted to be ill any more, there would be much less illness. There are so many cases of people afflicted with the same illness, some with neither the time nor the wish to be ill, and others enjoying their illness to the full, keeping their temperature up day after day. I believe very strongly in the possibility of having a temperature, of starting off illnesses oneself and misleading the doctor. . . .

"I hate health, because health is council flats, traffic jams and all that kind of thing. Illness is the opposite. Health is the law, the vital minimum, health administered by society is a makeshift, it's the daily grind . . . it's a kind of slow poisoning . . . Health is what is required of you every day, and that's why one isn't particularly anxious to get better, because health is such a dull thing that if, from time to time, there weren't the holidays provided by illness, or just holidays. . . .

"It's a life outside life, it's an interim period when you have the right to develop all the things within you, knowing that you will afterwards have to start again, that that will be finished. I think this is the most honest way of looking at it, but illness is something you must live for yourself and not for others. When your everyday life affects others, when the mother of a family has to say, 'But what will my children do if I am ill', she can no longer bear to be ill. Illness itself, here, is poisoned by everyday life. It's no longer a genuine illness now, it's a problem which prevents other people from being happy. Now, from this point of view, it's something quite unbearable, perhaps worse than the seriousness of the illness itself or the fear of dying. It's a case of, 'The others won't be able to get on without me'. The illness of the person who, in life, does not live for herself but for others, is not for her any more. The person who lives so that others may live can't any longer afford a real illness . . . it's a kind of solitary pleasure, illness."

Illness as an occupation

Mme C, 54 years of age

"I've had very considerable experience of illness, I've had a lot of operations, you know, very great experience . . . quite enough, since I had cancer, three and a half years ago, and do you know, I believe I've still got it because it's the kind of thing you don't get rid of it until you give up, and you know what that means. So, I think I live with it and, you know, I don't live badly. I was full of life before, very dynamic. I still am, but mostly verbally, because in fact, I often feel exhausted. But you know, I started work again, and now I stop when I feel I can't do any more. . . .

"It showed itself, as it generally shows itself, by a lump on the breast, and the doctor didn't believe it was. He told me, 'It's nothing', and I had this lump for ten months; that shows that he was slow off the mark. Only, I was losing weight all the time, I was all in. Well, I wanted to know definitely what was the matter with me and of course, every time I saw the doctor's face close . . . or else they were extremely condescending, you know, kind and brotherly. I know quite well what that means, and then, all of a sudden, 'We'll have to operate . . . we'll have to operate this evening, that's what; do you want to live or die?' . . .

"When it's like that, you want first to know, and also you want to try everything. To have a breast removed, for a woman, is a very distressing thing . . . I don't know why, it's something I was very, very afraid of and I said to myself, 'Well, I'll find out first, and I won't do just anything . . .' I went my own way, except for a doctor to whom I certainly owe a lot, who told me, 'I'm not in favour of operation . . . anyway, I'll have to see what you've got; I'll have to make an examination, what's called a biopsy.' That's really no joke, because I had an internal haemorrhage of the breast, a haematoma, I went around for a month with a drainage tube in my breast, doing my shopping just the same. He told me the truth because he saw I had to know. I said to him, 'I have a little girl, I'm alone, I want to know the truth. Am I good for two months, for six months, for a year? . . .'

"Well, I'd never felt better. I had the feeling that I was free of all that nonsense, and that I was face to face with something. When I'm face to face with something, I can put up a very good fight. I think it's not a bad thing to know, provided you have a minimum of courage.

I'm not so very brave, in fact, I'm rather a coward . . . but in things like that, you have to do something, you have to put up a fight. Now, as for my state of mind, if you're interested, well, I've lived with death all the time, admitting it, and finding it wasn't as dreadful as all that. I thought I'd have a lot of difficulty, but . . . I put up a fight so that it hasn't been too bad. Now, I've resumed work, I stop when I'm tired, I live like many other women of 50. . . .

"It shakes you . . . when you have something like that, at first, you really feel shaken . . . only, if you get over it, it's the best experience in the world. I very much wanted to get better, first because I wanted to show others that you could get better, and so, in the nursing homes, I was always talking about it. Once I got scolded because I had spoken of it. I said, 'No, I'm not speaking about it in order to speak about myself, but to tell them to look at me.' It's very nice, if you get over it, to be able to tell the others and encourage them . . . but all the same, it's quite a thing to wake up one day with cancer. It's not a trivial thing, when you think of it, it's really hard. . . .

"I've had migraines all my life, and a whole lot of things, crying when I had serious family problems, emotional problems with my daughter's father, really being flayed alive. And then, one day, when I had a blow like this, I learned above all that first, you don't have time to waste, and then there are some things which matter and others which don't, and then, it isn't important if I die, it isn't serious; the only thing that's necessary is to have foreseen it so that no harm can come to my little girl. For her, also, I fought hard, it was a fight all the time, all the time. It was very expensive looking after myself; I had to take a taxi every day to the American hospital and back; that cost a lot, 40,000 francs a month. I had awful times having ray treatment, that's really hard . . . and then, there I saw ever so many people who were afflicted, who didn't know what they had, it was awful to see them. The times when it was especially hard were and still are, every time I go to the doctor to ask how I'm getting on. Every time, before seeing him, I am ill for three days, I wonder, 'What's he going to say to me?' because I know he won't lie to me, and anyway, if he lied, I'd be sure to see it straight away because now I know him well. You know, I'm scared just the same, I am, everybody is . . . but you know, you live with it . . . I think everyone who has something wrong with him lives with his ailment . . .

"I have a friend who is paralysed from the shoulders down. She had a fall and there's nothing can be done, she's permanently paralysed . . .

She said to me one day, 'Illness is an occupation.' Now I know it's an occupation too, only, I'd say that for me, it's more of an occupation when I can put up a fight against my illness. Now, I no longer fight because I'm working, I haven't the time. So at present, it's more or less on its own, it's annoying. I don't have time to treat my illness with due respect because I have too much to do, too much work. . . .

"Also, when you have cancer, many sources of comfort are forbidden, especially stimulants which may make the cells multiply. Even a cup of coffee is bad for me. My digestion's upset after the rays, I have quite serious stomach trouble. Formerly, I had a reserve of health . . . I had really an extraordinary reserve of health which enabled me to react to anything; quite simply, I react less effectively . . . I curl up and wait till it passes and I avoid stimulants because I really feel that they have a much more toxic effect than they used to have. . . .

"I'm terribly afraid of illness, I hate illness, but you know as far as I'm concerned, it's rather like having a double with me now, I've got to accept it, I can't get rid of it. Well, obviously, for those who knew me formerly, it must be distressing for them. I had friends who came to my bedside, and I thought, 'I'm going to be something repulsive now.' Well, I had friends who came and drank from my glass to show me that they still liked me . . . that's not meaningless, it's one of the things that restored my morale. In truth, I haven't changed much, I've got very old and very fat, but you know, I don't think I give the impression of being in poor health. . . .

"Well, there you are, it's not such a terribly serious illness if you get over it . . . cancer . . . it's a dreadful word, it's a word which frightens people. Only, when you have it yourself, you say to yourself, 'I'm an invalid, like my neighbour who has chronic bronchitis!' . . .

"I think it's better, though, to know what you're up against. Lots of people prefer not to know, they're afraid of it as if it were something disgraceful . . . but when it concerns your near relatives, people look after their near relatives, and realize that it's the same face and the same hands. . . .

"However terrible life may be, if I could start it again, I'd start it again with cancer . . . it hasn't taken away my taste for life at all. All invalids love life, they aren't people without hope."

Bibliography

Allendy, R. (1944). " Journal d'un Médecin Malade". Denoël, Paris.

Apple, D. (1960). "How Laymen Define Illness". *J. Health Hum. Behav.* **1**, 219–225.

Balint, M. (1957). "The Doctor, his Patient and the Illness". Pitman, London.

Barker, R. G., Wright, B. A. and Gonick, M. B. (Revised 1953). "Adjustment to Physical Handicap and Illness. A Survey of the Social Psychology of Physique and Disability". Social Science Research Council Bull. 55, New York.

Bastide, R. (1965). "Sociologie des Maladies Mentales". Flammarion, Paris.

Baumann, B. (1961). Diversities in conceptions of health and physical fitness. *J. Health Hum. Behav.* **2**, 39–46.

Canguilhem, G. (1950). "Essai sur Quelques Problemes Concernant le Normal et le Pathologique". 2nd ed. Les Belles Lettres, Paris.

Cannon, W. B. (1944). Voodoo death. *Amer Anthrop.* **42**, 169–181.

Carstairs, G. M. (1955). Medicine and faith in rural Rajasthan, *in* "Health, Culture and Community. Case Studies of Public Reactions to Health Programs". pp. 107–134. (Eds B. D. Paul and W. B. Miller), Russell Sage Foundation, New York.

Chombart De Lauwe, P. H. *et al.* (1963). "La Femme dans la Société. Son Image Dans Différents Milieux Sociaux". Editions du C.N.R.S., Paris.

Clausen, J. A. (1959). The sociology of mental illness, *in* "Sociology Today" (Eds R. K. Merton *et al.*). Basic Books, New York.

Clements, F. (1932). Primitive concepts of disease. *Pub. Amer. Arch. Ethn.* **32**, 185–252·

Cobb, B. (1958). Why do people detour to quacks? *in* "Patients, Physicians and Illness. Sourcebook in Behavioural Science and Medicine" (Ed E. G. Jaco.). The Free Press, Glencoe, Illinois.

Davis, F. (1960). Uncertainty in medical prognosis, clinical and functional. *Amer. J. Soc.* **66**, 41–47.

Dubos, R. (1961). Mirage de la Santé. French translation, Denoël, Paris.

Faris, R. E. L. and Dunham, H. W. (1939). "Mental Disorders in Urban Areas". University of Chicago Press, Chicago.

Foucault, M. (1963). "Naissance de la Clinique. Une Archéologie du Regard Médical". Presses Universitaires de France, Paris.

Foucault, M. (1961). "Folie et Deraison. Histoire de la Folie à l'age Classique". Plon, Paris.

Fox, R. C. (1959). "Experiment Perilous: Physicians and Patients Facing the Unknown". The Free Press, Glencoe, Illinois.

Frake, C. O. (1961). The diagnostic of disease among the Subanum of Mindano. *Amer. Anthropol.* **63**, 113–132.

Freidson, E. (1960). Client control and medical practice. *Amer. J. Sociol.* **65**, 374–382.

Freidson, E. (1961). "Patients' Views of Medical Practice – a Study of Subscribers to a Prepaid Medical Plan in the Bronx". Russell Sage Foundation, New York.

Freidson, E. (1961–62). The sociology of medicine. A trend report and bibliography. *Current Sociology*, 10–11.

Freud, S. (1964). Thoughts for the times on war and death, *in* "Complete Psychological Works", Standard edition, vol. 14. Hogarth Press, London.

Goldstein, B. and Dommermuth, P. (1961). The sick-role cycle: an approach to medical sociology. *Soc. Soc. Res.* **47**, 1–12.

Goldstein, B. and Eichhorn, R. L. (1661). The changing protestant ethic: rural patterns in health, work and leisure. *Amer. Sociol. Rev.* **26**, 556–565.

Gould, H. A. (1957). The implication of technological change for folk and scientific medicine. *Amer. Anthropol.* **29**, 507–519.

Gourevitch, M. (1964). Esquisse d'une mythologie de la santé et de la maladie. *L'encephale*, 437–477.

Graham, S. (1963). Social factors in relation to chronic illness, *in* "Handbook of Medical Sociology" (Eds M. E. Freeman, S. Levine and L. G. Reeder). Prentice-Hall, Englewood Cliffs, N.J.

Green, A. L. (1961). Ideology of anti-fluoridation leaders. *J. Soc. Issues*, **17**, 13–25.

Hoffer, C. and Schuler, E. (1948). Measurement of health needs and health care. *Amer. Sociol. Rev.* **13**, 719–724.

Hollingshead, A. B. and Redlich, F. C. (1958). "Social Class and Mental Illness". John Wiley, New York.

Jahoda, M. (1953). The meaning of psychological health. *Social Casework* (Family Service Association of America).

Kaes, R. (1966). "La Culture. Son Image Chez les Ouvriers Français". Faculté des Lettres et Sciences Humaines de Paris, Nanterre.

Koos, E. L. (1960). Illness in Regionville, *in* "Sociological Studies of Health and Sickness" (Ed. D. Apple). McGraw Hill, New York.

Kubie, L. S. (1954). The fundamental nature of the distinction between normality and neurosis. *Psychoanal. Quarterly*, **23**, 167–204.

Lamy, M. (1964). "Où en est la médicine?" Flammarion, Paris.

Lederer, H. D. (1952). How the sick view their world, *J. Soc. Issues*, **7** (4), 4–15.

Leriche, R. (1936). De la santé à la maladie, *in* "Encyclopédie Française."

Mauss, M. (1950). Effet physique chez l'individu de l'idée de mort suggérée par la collectivité (1926), *in* "Sociologie et Anthropologie", Presses Universitaires de France, Paris.

Mead, Margaret (ed.) (1954). "Cultural Patterns and Technical Change". Unesco, Paris; Columbia University Press. New York.

Mechanic, D. (1960). The concept of illness behaviour. *J. Chron. Dis.* **15**, 189–194.

Mechanic, D. (1968). "Medical Sociology, a Selective View". The Free Press, New York.

Mechanic, D. and Volkart, E. H. (1961) Stress, illness behaviour and the sick role. *Amer. Sociol. Rev.* **26,** 51–58.

Moscovici, S. (1961). La Psychanalyse, son Image et son Public. Etude sur la Représentation Sociale de la Psychanalyse". Presses Universitaires de France, Paris.

Osgood, C. E. (1959). The representational model, *in* "Trends in Content Analysis" (Ed I-de Sola Pool), University of Illinois Press, Urbana, Illinois.

Parsons, T. (1951). Social structure and dynamic process: the case of modern medical practice, *in* "The Social System", pp. 428–480. The Free Press, Glencoe, Illinois.

Parsons, T. (1958). Definitions of health and illness in the light of American values and social structure, *in* "Patients, Physicians and Illness" (Ed E. G. Jaco), pp. 165–187. The Free Press, Glencoe, Illinois.

Phillips, E. L. (1965). Self reliance and the inclination to adopt the sick role. *Soc. Forces,* **43,** 222–263.

Pratt, L. (1956). How do patients learn about disease? *Soc. Problems,* **4,** 29–40.

Pratt, L. Seligman, A. and Reader, G. (1958). Physicians' views on the level of medical information among patients, *in* "Patients, Physicians and Illness" (Ed E. G. Jaco). The Free Press, Glencoe, Illinois.

Redlich, F. C. (1957). The concept of health in psychiatry, *in* "Explorations in Social Psychiatry" (Eds A. H. Leighton, J. A. Clausen and R. N. Wilson). Basic Books, New York.

Rivers, W. H. R. (1924). "Medicine, Magic and Religion". Kegan Paul, London.

Rousseau, J-J. (1913). "The Social Contract Discourses". Everyman's Library, Dent, London.

Ruesch, J. (1953). Social technique, social status and social change in illness, *in* "Personality in Nature, Society and Culture" (Eds C. Kluckhohn and H. A. Murray), 2nd edition. Knopf, New York.

Saunders, L. (1959). "Cultural Differences and Medical Care". Russell Sage Foundation, New York.

Schwartz, C. G. (1957). Perspectives on deviance – wives' definitions of their husbands' mental illness. *Psychiatry,* **20,** 275–291.

Selye, H. (1956). "The Stress of Life". McGraw Hill, New York.

Shryock, R. H. (1947). "Histoire de la Médicine Moderne". Armand Colin, Paris.

Sigerist, H. E. (1943). "Civilization and Disease". University of Chicago Press, Chicago.

Sigerist, H. E. (1955). "A History of Medicine", 2nd edition. Oxford University Press, New York.

Stoetzel, J. (1960). La maladie, le malade et le médicin, esquisse d'une analyse psychosociale. *Population,* **12,** 613–624.

Strauss, R. (1957). The nature and status of medical sociology. *Amer. Sociol. Rev.* **22,** 200–204.

Suchman, E. (1964). Sociomedical variations among ethnic groups. *Amer. J. Sociol.* **70,** 319–331.

Valabrega, J. P. (1962). "La Relation Thérapeutique. Malade et Médecin". Flammarion, Paris.

Whiteman, M. and Lukoff, I. F. (1965). Attitude toward blindness and other physical handicaps. *J. Soc. Psychol.* **66,** 133–145.

Yarrow, M. R. *et al.* (1960). The psychological meaning of mental illness in the family, *in* "Sociological Studies of Health and Sickness" (Ed. D. Apple), pp. 56–68. McGraw Hill, New York.

Author Index

Numbers in italics refer to pages where references are listed at the ends of chapters

A
Allendy, R., 134, *151*
Apple, D., 10, *151*

B
Balint, M., 8, 49, 79, 83, 126, *151*
Barker, R. G., 7, 8, 126, *151*
Bastide, R., 7, 139, *151*
Baumann, B., 10, *151*
Bernard, C., 73
Brissaud, 79

C
Canguilhem, G., 6, 55, 60, 61, 62, 83, 86, *151*
Cannon, W. B., 138, *151*
Carstairs, G. M., 5, *151*
Chombart de Lauwe, P. H., 10, *151*
Clausen, J. A., 129, *151*
Clements, F., 5, *151*
Cobb, B., 129, *151*
Comte, A., 73

D
Davis, F., 135, *151*
Denoël, A., 134, *151*
Domermuth, P., 7, *152*
Dubos, R., 3, 31, *151*
Dunham, H. W., 7, *151*

E
Eichhorn, R. L., 126, *152*

F
Faris, R. E. L., 7, *151*
Foucault, M., 6, *151*
Fox, R. C., 127, *151*
Frake, C. O., 65, *152*
Freidson, E., 9, 10, *152*
Freud, S., 76, *152*

G
Goldstein, B., 7, 126, *152*
Gonick, M. B., 7, 8, 126, *151*

Gould, H. A., 5, *152*
Gourevitch, M., 134, 135, *152*
Graham, S., 7, *152*
Green, A. L., 41, *152*

H
Hippocrates, 2
Hirsch, A., 3
Hoffer, C., 84, *152*
Hollingshead, A. B., 7, *152*

J
Jahoda, M., 55, *152*
Jenner, L., 31

K
Kaes, R., 10, *152*
Koos, E. L., 84, *152*
Kubie, L. S., 55, *152*

L
Lamy, M., 48, *152*
Lederer, H. D., 7, 126, *152*
Leriche, R., 69, 83, *152*
Lukoff, J. F., 138, *154*

M
Mauss, M., 137, 138, *152*
Mead, Margaret, 5, *152*
Mechanic, D., 7, 9, 84, 85, *152, 153*
Moscovici, S., 10, 60, 137, *153*

N
Nicolle, C., 48

O
Osgood, C. E., 15, *153*

P
Paracelsus, 2
Parsons, T., 8, 104, 129, *153*
Pasteur, L., 5
Phillips, E. L., 126, *153*
Pratt, L., 84, *153*

155

R

Reader, G., 84, *153*
Redlich, F. C., 7, 55, *152, 153*
Rivers, W. H. R., 4, *153*
Rousseau, J-J., 31, *153*
Ruesch, J., 7, *153*

S

Saunders, L., 5, *153*
Schuler, E., 84, *152*
Schwartz, C. G., 126, *153*
Seligman, A., 84, *153*
Selye, H., 7, *153*
Shryock, R. H., 6, *153*
Sigerist, H. E., 2, 3, 4, 6, *153*

Stoetzel, J., 5, 8, 49, 60, 84, *153*
Strauss, R., 6, *153*
Suchman, E., 84, *153*

V

Valabrega, J. P., 2, 4, 6, 55, 76, 85, 129, *153*
Volkart, E. H., 9, 84, 85, *153*

W

Whiteman, M., 138, *153*
Wright, B. A., 7, 8, 126, *151*

Y

Yarrow, M. R., 126, *154*

Subject Index

A

Acceptance, 127
Accommodation, 44
Accidents, 65–66, 68
Acculturation, 5
Achievement, 127
Activity, 42, 63, 70, 82, 87, 91, 93–94, 107, 123, 125–126, 128–129, 132, 136, 137, 139
Adaptation, 44
Adjustment, 93, 96, 125
Air, 33, 45, 98
Alienation, 41, 97
Ambivalence, 111
Anatomy, 2
Anchorage, 137
Annihilation, 108–109, 113, 120, 123, 128, 132
Anthropology, 3, 4ff, 12
Anticipation, 44
Anxiety, 21, 108, 123
Asceticism, 126
Assimilation, 44, 63, 99
"Attenuation", 109
Attitudes, 9, 11, 94ff, 118, 126–127, 138–139
Autonomy, 126

B

Behaviour, 7, 9ff, 34, 74–75, 85–86, 93ff, 98, 111, 117, 127, 129, 131, 133–134, 139, 141
Behaviour
adaptive, 9
regressive, 9

C

Cancer, 22, 33, 67, 76, 95, 120, 124
Categories,
choice of, 15
Chemistry, 2
Cleanliness, 98
Communication, 11, 22, 94, 98, 108, 117, 124, 135
Conflict, 29, 47, 50, 72, 93, 97, 138

Conformity, 104, 130
Consciousness, 4
Consensus, 11
Constitution, 23, 26, 48
Constraint, 8, 28ff, 36, 38ff, 97, 102ff, 114, 116–117, 120, 137–139
Culture, 3

D

Death, 75ff, 108, 115, 128, 137–138
Defence, 86, 138
Dependence, 108
"Depersonalization", 110, 124
Depression, 69–70
Desocialization, 105–106, 115, 118–119
Destructive illness, 105ff, 115, 117–118, 120ff, 124, 126–127, 129, 131–132, 142ff
Deviance, 8–9, 12, 104, 107–108, 116, 125, 130ff, 139
Disease,
endogenous and exogenous conceptions of, 4–5, 19, 30, 48
predisposition to, 5, 19, 23, 25, 48
Disequilibrium, 2, 29
Disintegration,
personal, 107

E

Eating, 97–98, 101
Ego, 8
Egocentrism, 126
Epidemiology, 6–7
Equilibrium, 8, 20, 36, 55, 58ff, 66, 69–70, 72, 82, 95, 121, 129, 130
Exclusion, 104ff, 108, 113, 115, 127, 136–137

F

Fatigue, 20–21, 46–47, 69ff, 74, 79, 122
Fear, 123
Fixation, 109
Food, 32ff, 98, 101–102

G

Germs, 21
Guilt, 50

H

Health,
  concept of, 55ff
"Health-in-a-vacuum", 55–56, 58–59, 62–
  63, 72
Health,
  perfect, 62
  reserve of, 55ff, 61, 63, 91, 103, 122
Health behaviours, 101
Health measures, 100ff
"Health paradox", 102
Heart disease, 22
Heredity, 5, 19, 21, 25–26
Holidays, 98, 114, 116
Hospital, 1, 7, 108
Hygiene, 3, 5, 95ff
Hygiene behaviour, 94
Hypochondriacs, 86

I

Identity, 125 126ff, 139
Illness,
  benign, 76, 110
  as an occupation, 111, 119ff, 126, 128ff,
    142, 148ff
  as a liberator, 114ff, 121–122, 124, 126ff,
    139, 142, 145ff
  "behaviour", 7, 9, 85, 94, 104, 127,
    133, 137, 139
  conceptions of, 104ff
  curable, 66–67
  denial of, 120, 126–127, 129, 132–133,
    136
  duration of, 66ff, 111, 113
  fatal, 75
  localization of, 77, 135
  medical conceptions of, 82
  phases of, 7
  resistance to, 5, 19, 21, 24, 26, 30, 39,
    47, 50, 57, 63, 99, 134
  serious, 66–67, 75
  stages in, 7
Illnesses, 65ff, 85
  classifications of, 65ff
Impotence, 111
Inactivity, 74, 77–78, 80ff, 85, 87, 91, 94,
  104ff, 110, 119–120, 128, 132, 136–
  137
Independence, 109
Individualism, 126
Influenza, 67
"Institutionalized anticipations", 104

Integration, 96, 127, 130
"Intermediate state", 20–21, 23, 47, 50,
  69ff, 74
Introversion, 126
Introversive tendencies, 8
Invalid autism, 108
Isolation, 81

M

Magic, 5
Maladjustment, 2
Malaise, 46, 47, 69
Medical beliefs, 4
Medical geography, 3
Medical practice, 4
Medicine,
  Greek, 6
  humanization of, 6
  modern, 83
  psychosomatic, 3
  primitive, 4
  scientific, 2, 5
  social, 3
  sociology in, 6
  sociology of, 3–4, 6
  western, 4
Mental disorder, 22
Migraine, 71
Models,
  cultural, 1

N

"Nerves",
  nervousness, 20–21, 45–46, 70
Noise, 42
Norms, 1, 9ff, 62–63, 70, 86, 102ff, 129,
  130–131, 136, 139

O

Observation,
  methods of, 13, 16
Occupations,
  sociology of, 7
Omnipotence, 111

P

Pain, 65ff, 77, 81, 111, 115, 120, 122
Participation, 104ff, 121–122, 128, 131,
  136
Passivity, 112–113, 132
Pathology, 3, 73
Personality, 94, 106–107, 109, 111, 116–
  117, 124, 138, 141
  enrichment of, 117
Physical impairment, 111
Physics, 2

Physiology, 2
Pneumonia, 110
Poliomyelitis, 66
Prescriptions, 1
Propaganda, 43
Psychiatry,
   social, 3
Psychoanalysis, 8, 10

R

Reality,
   physical, 83
   social, 3, 10, 11
Receptivity, 117
Regression, 109, 129
Regressive tendencies, 8
Relations,
   interpersonal, 7
   patient–doctor, 79, 86, 123
Relativity,
   cultural, 3
Relaxation, 28, 98, 101
Religion, 5
Representations, 4–5, 10ff, 26, 28, 36,
   39, 56, 60, 77, 82, 85, 91ff, 110, 131,
   138
Responsibility, 8, 50, 106, 117–117 128,
   138, 139
Rhythm (of life), 28, 31, 33–34, 36
Role, 1, 9ff, 105ff, 116, 118, 120, 122,
   130
   doctor's, 8–9
   patient's, 8
Rules, 1, 101, 103

S

Science,
   medical, 6
Self concept, 130–131
Self definition, 127
Self expression, 127
Semantic differential, 138
"Sick role", 9, 104, 123, 126–127, 130, 132
Sleep, 98
Social class, 7
Social definition, 1, 9

Social expectations, 9, 130
Social integration, 118
Social object, 12
Social obligations, 114–115, 119
Social Security, 1
Social status, 81, 109
Social structure, 2
Social system, 104, 130
Social universe, 107
Society, 1, 3, 5–6, 9–10, 12, 28, 30–31, 37–
   38, 41, 49, 85, 91 93–94, 104, 116,
   118–119, 125, 127ff, 132, 136ff
   primitive, 4
Sociology, 6
Solitude, 106, 115, 119
Sports, 101
Stress, 7
Suffering, 108, 124
Superstition, 4
Symptoms, 76, 78–79, 83

T

Temperament, 24, 26, 124
Temperature, 76, 79, 111, 118, 122
Tension, 20–21, 43, 50
Toxicity, 41ff, 47
Tuberculosis, 66–67, 76, 79, 112, 115
Typhoid, 110

U

Unconscious, 13
Units of analysis,
   choice of, 15
Utopia, 96

V

Values, 1, 3, 5, 11, 97, 121, 125–126, 139

W

"Way of life", 19, 20ff, 25ff, 34–35, 37,
   42, 45ff, 91, 95, 97, 99ff, 134, 137–
   138
Will-power, 111
Work, 28
"World-without-illness", 14, 39, 116, 141

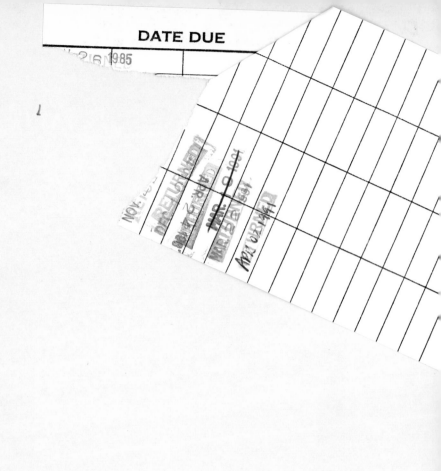